TOWARD A HOT JEW

FANTAGRAPHICS BOOKS

Editor: Gary Groth
Designer: Keeli McCarthy
Production: Paul Baresh
Editorial Assistance: RJ Casey
Publisher: Gary Groth

F.U. Press
7563 Lake City Way NE
Seattle, Washington 98115

First F.U. Press edition: September 2016
ISBN 978-1-60699-981-3
Printed in Korea. FU008

TOWARD

A

HOT

Graphic essays by Miriam Libicki

JEW

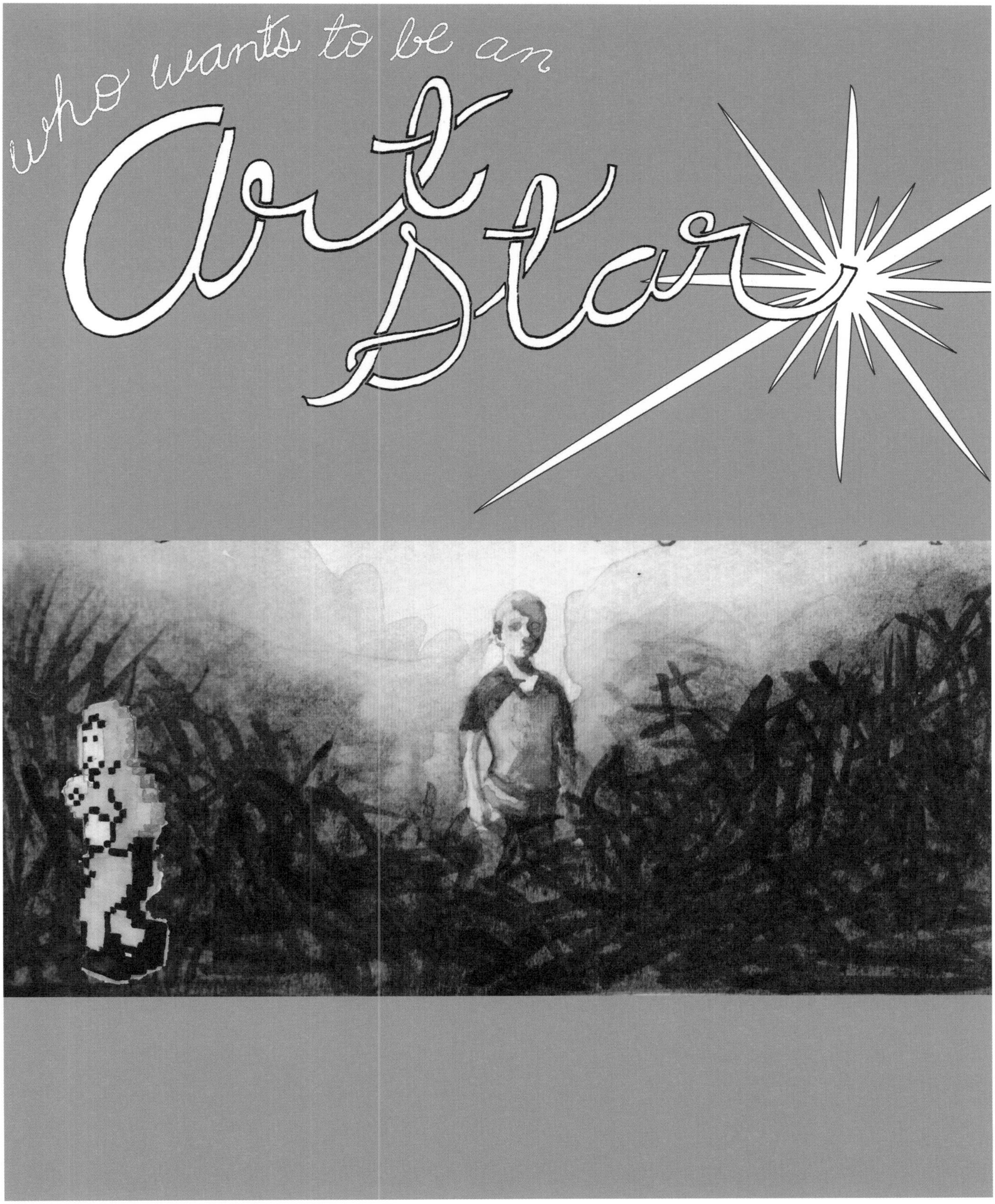
who wants to be an
Art
Star

I enrolled at the Emily Carr Institute of Art & Design in 2003. Initially, I'd wanted to be a children's book illustrator. During my first course there, I started drawing comics stories & wanted to continue that. But since the school didn't have an illustration or a comics department, I was officially a Visual Arts major, with a concentration on painting & drawing.

Still I felt lucky to be in their world, in their classes & sharing their studio space. Especially in third year, when everyone stopped being in shock over the university setting, & seemed to be 'finding their voices' as painters.

Our painting 310 instructor in Fall 2004, Jordan Broadworth, gave us an assignment to 'have an art adventure': have some sort of extreme experience with art, then document it. Mine was to interview other students about their art adventures, & put them together as a comic. What follows is that comic, more or less.

I'm re-painting the pages, five years later, on the occasion of my return to the academic art scene. I've been a working cartoonist since just before graduating. This fall, I'll be teaching a comic course at Emily Carr.

I thought it would be interesting now to relive being a student, trying to decide what Art meant to the world, & what you meant to the Art World.

I really enjoyed my time as a spectator in that world of giant canvases that were tacked on the wall of your studio space at the beginning of each semester & never really finished, pulling 12+ hour days in the painting studios with short breaks for nicotine or pot, Making A Statement by painting your mom, or Dr. Zaius in the fashion of a Renaissance saint, keeping up on ArtForum to make sure your name-dropping was up-to-date for class critiques, going to weekly art openings to nod sagely at the walls & the artist's statement but above all, painting your freaking arms off.

For the parts I hated, such as artist's statements seeming to take precedence over the actual art in any show, I consoled myself that I wasn't gonna be a gallery-showing high artist. For the parts I envied, like the single-minded dedication of my painter peers that resulted in amazing beautiful paintings... I consoled myself that I wasn't gonna be a gallery-showing high artist.

I went around to friends here & asked them why they wanted to be artists.

It's a question that I ask myself, why do I paint what I do. I never really have an answer. I thought that if I asked other people, I might get closer to an answer for myself.

It was a difficult question for people to answer. Some people would just throw things out there, then give up & say they didn't know. Many people said that it was to express themselves, through forms, through colour.

One person said that for most of their life they were closed off to colour.

Then suddenly, everything became colourful.

& they had to show that.

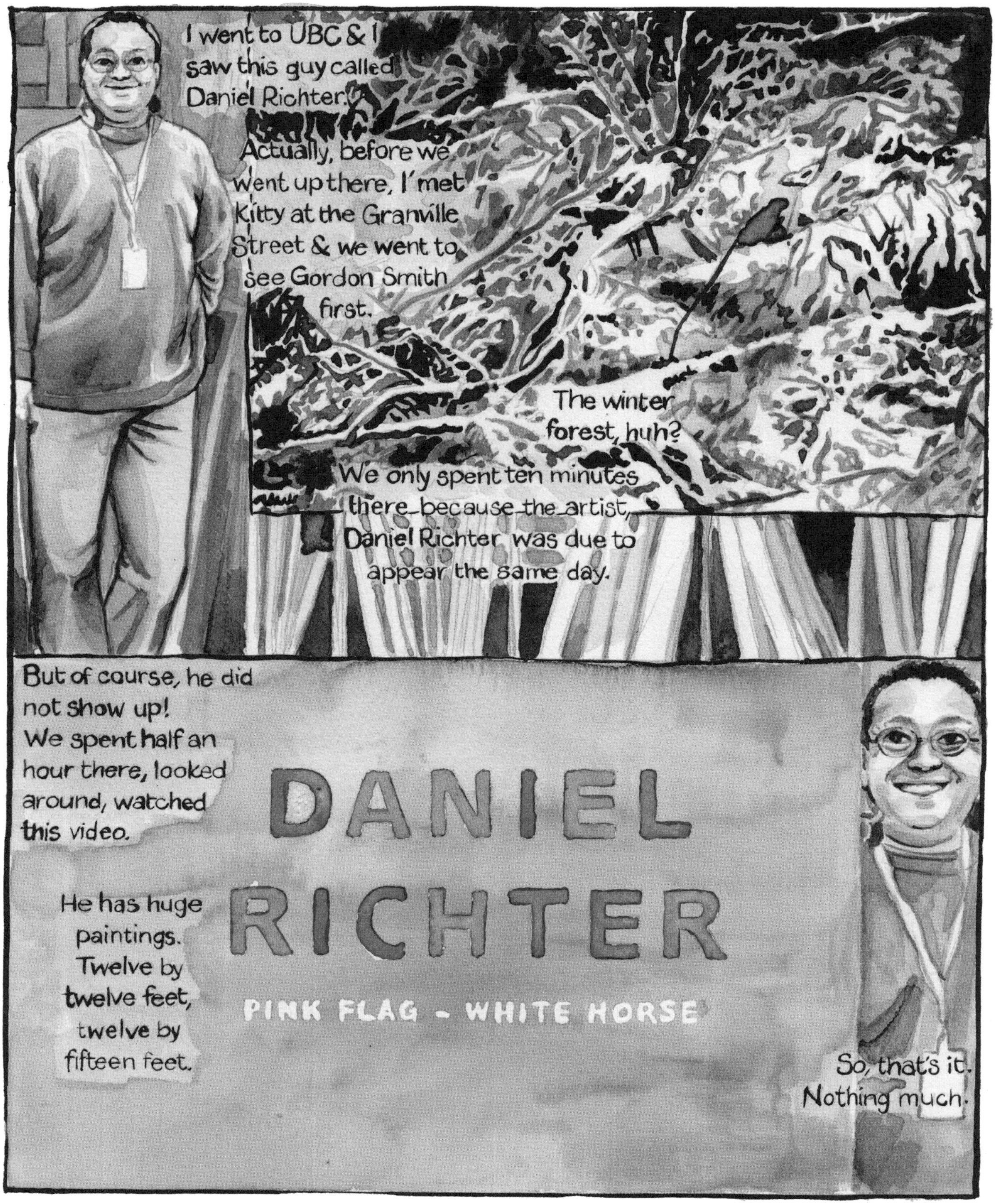
I went to UBC & I saw this guy called Daniel Richter.
Actually, before we went up there, I'met Kitty at the Granville Street & we went to see Gordon Smith first.
The winter forest, huh?
We only spent ten minutes there because the artist, Daniel Richter was due to appear the same day.
But of course, he did not show up! We spent half an hour there, looked around, watched this video.
DANIEL RICHTER
PINK FLAG - WHITE HORSE
He has huge paintings. Twelve by twelve feet, twelve by fifteen feet.
So, that's it. Nothing much.

I wrote about an old adventure, when I had an opening, & lots of people came & we got drunk.

I thought the opening was successful. I guess verbally expressing myself is difficult. I thought when people saw my paintings that I was expressing myself.

Brier Rose
Paintings by Jason Froese

Flower Factory
3604 Main St
Oct 9 - Nov. 3
Opening Thurs Oct 14, 7-9 pm

It was late & I was very drunk. I think I stepped on a dog on my way to get another beer.

The owner was cleaning up at the end & I stayed to talk with her. We talked about my statement & my pricing.

After that I decided not to stiff her on her share of the paintings I sold

What I wanted to look at was traditional gallery spaces, like four white walls.

I wanted to look at the more private, hidden spaces, the offices & storage rooms. I wanted to look at my own ideas of public & private.

In storage, paintings are looked at in bad light, stacked against each other. That's the personal.

I wonder if some paintings are made to be painted not seen, like a journal entry.

I thought I'd be dealing with just artwork, but I was more affected by the company I was with. You know, the girl?

That was the personal artwork.

Not the girl, but the relationship.

We were the private artwork in the public gallery space.

I kind of said it already in class. I'm going to take the Lil' Mac & do a stencil, & put him around the city in different interesting places.

I'd like to do it 3D, with a lot of foam cutouts so it wouldn't matter if people stole them. But I don't think I can do that right now.

The first part was a total failure. I wanted to go to daycares & see the kids' art, I'm interested in art without justification. But every place I called, people were freaked out, thinking I was a pervert.

the drunk people asked for cooler things, like outer space, my friend asked for ducks dancing.

My next idea was to ask a bunch of sober people what I should paint, & then get really fucked up & ask a bunch of similarly fucked up people.

The sober people asked for breasts, a penis, a naked waitress, a winning lottery ticket.

I was so fucked up though, I was writing these things down & I was hallucinating so bad I couldn't see the paper. It was hard reading some of the requests the next day.

The hardest one, I think I wrote "carburetor."

It wasn't exactly my idea.
The first idea was to do these interviews as a comic story.

I thought of journalistic comic books, like Joe Sacco's, or others that you start to see more often.

So to do something similar, I took photos of other people & interviewed them about their adventures.

I did it outside of class, just hanging around the painting studios looking for other students. There are some interviews I won't be able to use, cause people were in a hurry & I couldn't take pictures.

This will be a very different style of comic for me, being all photo-based, & the images don't really move along in the traditional narrative sense.

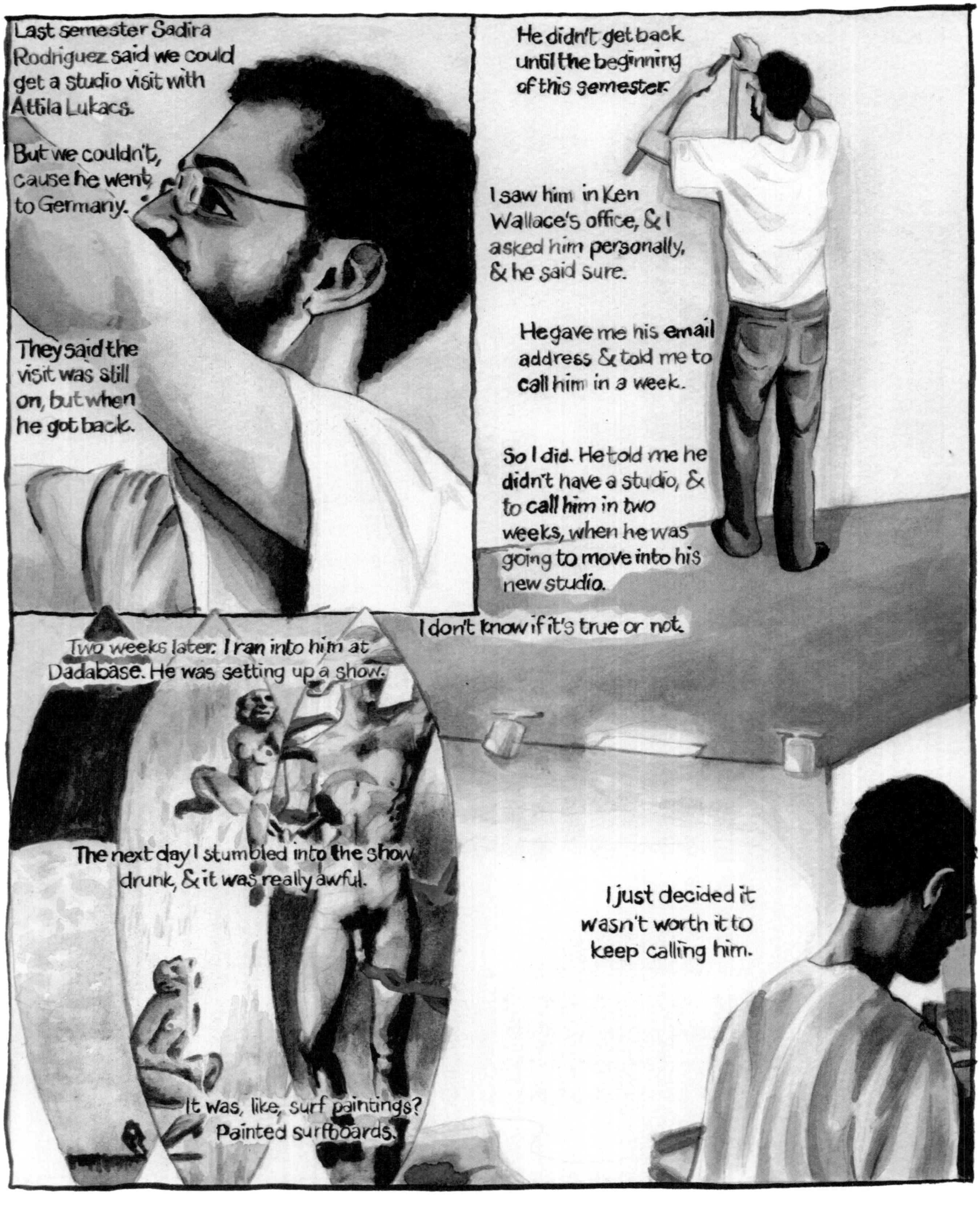
Last semester Sadira Rodriguez said we could get a studio visit with Attila Lukacs.
But we couldn't, cause he went to Germany.
They said the visit was still on, but when he got back.
He didn't get back until the beginning of this semester.
I saw him in Ken Wallace's office, & I asked him personally, & he said sure.
He gave me his email address & told me to call him in a week.
So I did. He told me he didn't have a studio, & to call him in two weeks, when he was going to move into his new studio.
I don't know if it's true or not.
Two weeks later. I ran into him at Dadabase. He was setting up a show.
The next day I stumbled into the show drunk, & it was really awful.
It was, like, surf paintings? Painted surfboards.
I just decided it wasn't worth it to keep calling him.

Towards a Hot Jew
the Israeli soldier as fetish object

a drawn essay by Miriam Libicki

Although one of the streams of historical European anti-Semitism is a pronouncedly sexual one, the Jew in North American consciousness is curiously   unsexy, especially in Jewish eyes.

a joke:
"What do wives from different countries say during sex?

Italian : Oh, Giovanni, you are the world's greatest lover!

French : Ah, Pierre my darling, you are marvelous! More! More!

Jewish : Oy, Jake, the ceiling needs painting"
(Techno.co.il, an Israeli message board)

The North American stereotypes evolved, from the post-WWII influx of eastern European Jewish refugees, through the late '60s and '70s, when second-generation Jews rose to prominence in self-identified roles in popular culture.

The resulting ste-
reotypes which
cast men as weak
and neurotic and
women as
coldly materialis-
tic
"bears an uncanny
likeness to the
role of the entire
middle class in
the consumer
economy. The
middle
class in-
creasingly found
itself
anxious, passive,
and preyed
upon as
postwar
affluence
began to de-
cline in
the 1970s."
(Riv-Ellen Prell)

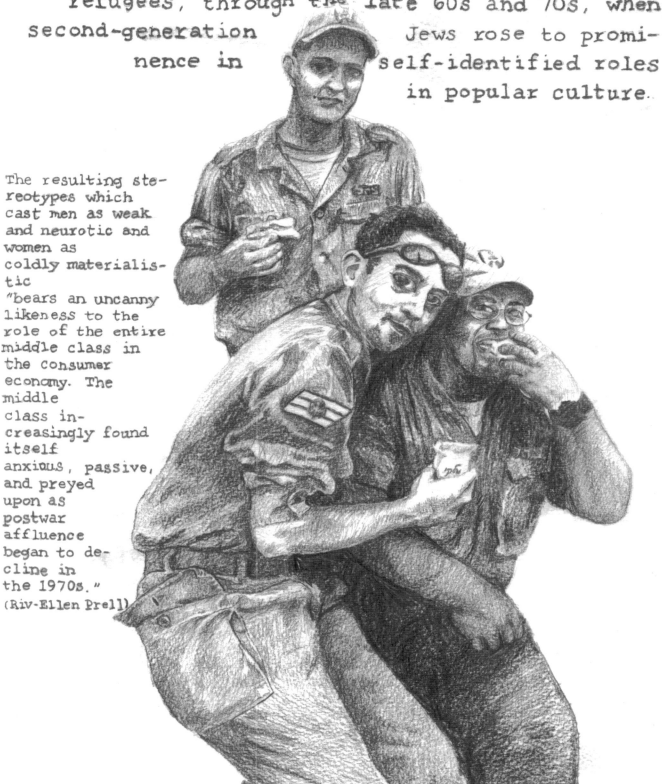

Even though it was often Jewish television writers creating Jewish television characters, "Jewish men on primetime television have assumed a plethora of negative or subordinated roles: passive fathers married to domineering, often vulgar Jewish women, nebbishy husbands and boyfriends involved with beautiful Gentile women, self-deprecating nerds, loyal side-kicks and cross-dressing effeminate men."
(Maurice Berger)

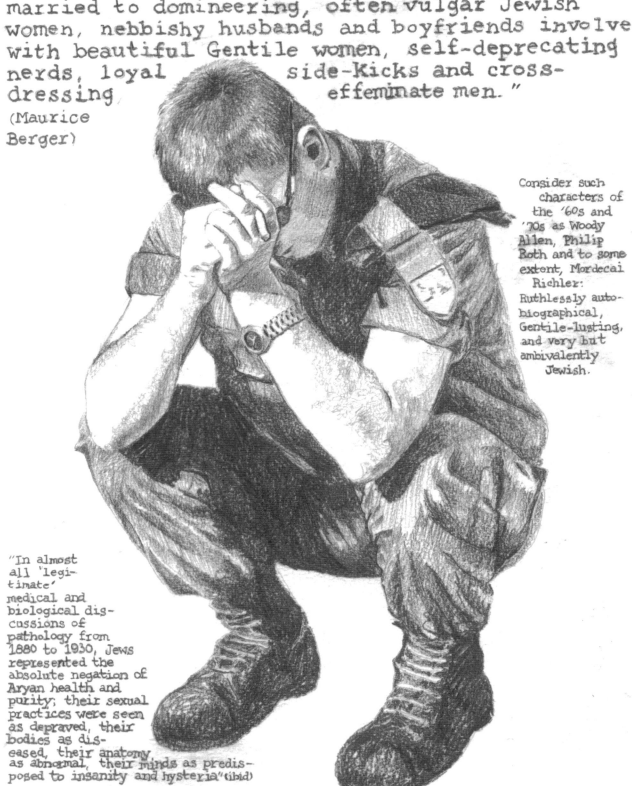

Consider such characters of the '60s and '70s as Woody Allen, Philip Roth and to some extent, Mordecai Richler: Ruthlessly auto-biographical, Gentile-lusting, and very but ambivalently Jewish.

"In almost all 'legitimate' medical and biological discussions of pathology from 1880 to 1930, Jews represented the absolute negation of Aryan health and purity; their sexual practices were seen as depraved, their bodies as diseased, their anatomy as abnormal, their minds as predisposed to insanity and hysteria" (ibid)

"The Jewish woman is represented through her body, which is at once exceptionally passive and highly adorned. She simultaneously lacks sexual desire____ and lavishes attention on beautifying herself." (Riv-Ellen Prell)

The term Jewish American Princess ("JAP") gained currency in the '70s. I don't know if there's a Canadian equivalent.

a joke:
"The scene is in bed.
He: can I do anything?
She: sure, as long as you don't touch my hair." (ibid)

Many Jewish movements, from Enlightenment onwards, have tried to substitute new images, "muscular Jews," for negative stereotypes. This photo, and Israel's 1967 war, may have finally done it.

These are Israeli paratroopers, young, tough, virile, looking with religious awe at the freshly conquered Western Wall

Strong yet humble, freed from oppressive religion yet full of identification with heritage, not to mention blonde!

This image, and the war behind it, ushered in both the muscular Jew and the occupied Palestinian territories, where these muscles are shown exercised to extremes.

The new image was so powerful that North American Jewish parents, from the '70s onward, have sent their teenagers on Israel trips (two weeks to a year post high school) to cement sympathy with the Jewish State and plant the idea that Jews are kinda hot.

"I think Israel would be a great place for me to live and find a partner. There's nowhere else I feel so comfortable as a gay man and a Jew. I tried to buy an Israeli rainbow flag to hang out my window, but I kept getting distracted by all the cute soldiers."
(Jonathan Goler, Israel trip participant)

Jewish organizations fund youth trips to Israel and they explicitly state that one of their aims is to try to prevent youth from "marrying out" of Judaism... though I have had both the most cited vaccinations (going to Israel and attending Jewish private school) it is looking as if I will marry out.

It is always a welcome revelation.

Israeli Jews are more multi-ethnic than North American Jews, ingathering the exiles from Europe, North Africa, Ethiopia, the former Soviet Union, India, etc.

Being more varied, they are more exotic and less like the kids you grew up with.

"My short stint in Israel opened up a world of beauty to me (whilst simultaneously destroying my understanding of Jews as a united ethnic people, since we're so many damn ethnicities masquerading as this one umbrella label 'Jews'). Beauties from all over the world showcased the beauty of their own origins, from Persia to Germany to Morocco to Argentina to Mexico! I found the crowd of British girls at the girls' hostel next door to be ravishing: olive skin, long straight black hair, and oval features. I did not know this until walking around Jerusalem: freckles on a girl automatically make her an '8' in my book. Why hadn't I known Jews could be this sexy before?"
(Ben Murane, personal correspondence)

Given the odd visibility of Jews and the great interest of the US government in Israel, it didn't take long for the Israeli soldier to catch on in the Western media.

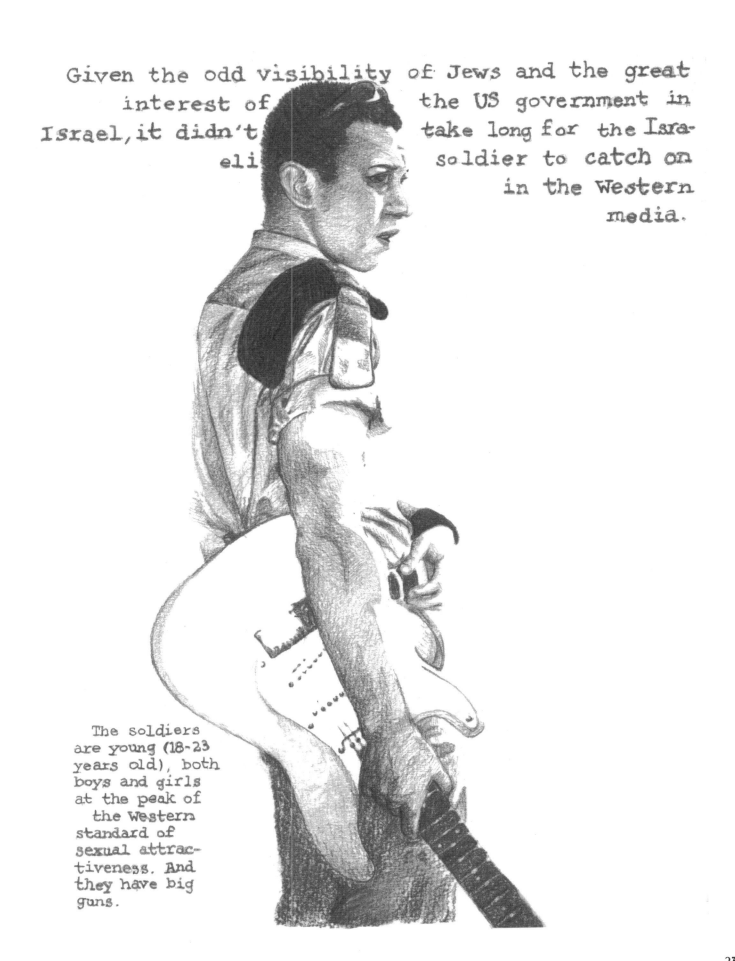

The soldiers are young (18-23 years old), both boys and girls at the peak of the Western standard of sexual attractiveness. And they have big guns.

Still? even post-Orientalism and intifada, when we know that Israel is the ultimate post-colonial/neo-colonial villain?

Israel is **almost** Western and **almost** a colonial power. Close enough, really.

Plus, there's this neat symmetry where Jews, the ultimate victims (Holocaust) are now the ultimate oppressors.

It makes great copy.

"Many of the methods of collective and individual 'punishment' meted out to Palestinian civilians at the hands of young, racist, often sadistic, and ever impervious Israeli soldiers at the hundreds of checkpoints littering the occupied Palestinian territories are reminiscent of common Nazi practices against the Jews." ("Peacepalestine", a blog)

But the image endures. The Israeli soldier is everywhere and sexier than ever.

In the West, where sexuality and sexual attraction are tied up with sin, shame and furtiveness, the person you are told to disapprove of is almost sexy by default.

Here I am thinking of such artists as Tom of Finland and Attila Richard Lukacs.

Also, of course, the oppressor/oppressed power struggle is infused with eroticism (and vice versa) in our postmodern conception.

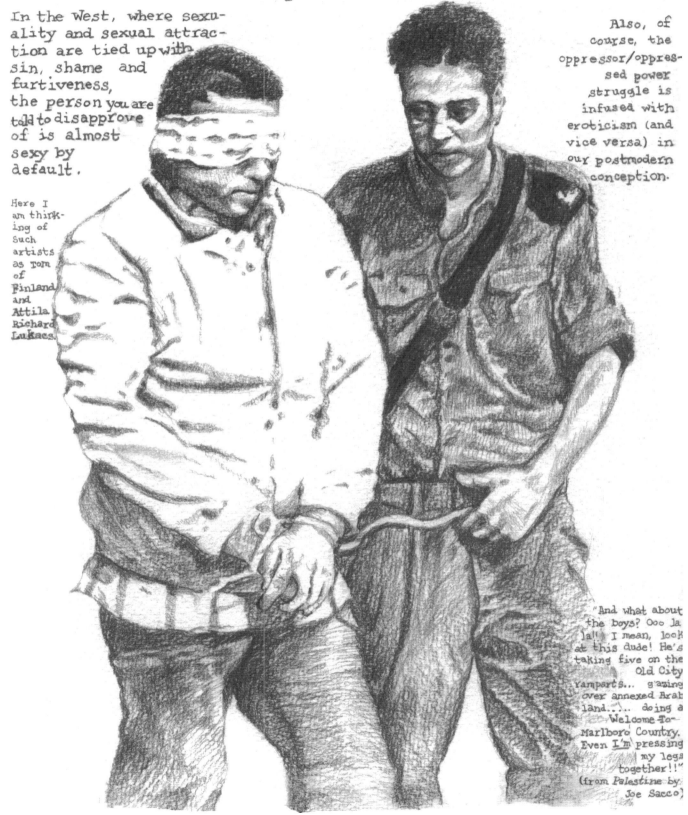

"And what about the boys? Ooo la la!! I mean, look at this dude! He's taking five on the Old City ramparts... gazing over annexed Arab land... doing a Welcome to Marlboro Country. Even I'm pressing my legs together!!" (from *Palestine* by Joe Sacco)

By the quirks of history, propaganda, and the voyeuristic urge, we have arrived at the New Jew: an adorable oppressor for every persuasion.

ceasefire

Israel
August 12-17
2006

August 10th

Little Samah is just one month old, but war is all she has ever known. Born in this cramped bomb shelter in Southern Lebanon, she and her family await the end of the shelling along with dozens of other families.

Her infant hair has already acquired a shock of white from the stress.

I have a one-month-old nephew. He's Israeli. In a few days I'm going from my home in Vancouver to Jerusalem, to meet him.

It looks like I couldn't have picked a worse time.

August 11th

My boyfriend's mum really doesn't want me to go.
She is Canadian. She says,

August 12th

The war with Hezbollah has been going on for just over a month. It looks very different from here than it did from Vancouver.

For one thing, nobody seems to think it is the beginning of World War Three.

Here it is seen as a way to get people to change their ISP (it rhymes in Hebrew).

August 13th

Ruti and her kids are residents of Haifa. They
  live on the top floor of their apartment
  building
    and have to go down to the basement
bomb
    shelter
        every time the air raid
    sirens go off.

My mother invited them down to
  my parents' empty house
    in Ashkelon, to get away for
              the weekend.

My parents are telling me it's
  ten times the sirens went off
      today! And I can't do
that,
  climb down over and over, with
              the baby.

We spend all afternoon
  at the beach nearby,
    and have ice
cream
        twice.

August 14th

On the phone with my boyfriend for the first time since I got here. His mother asks him if he's heard from me, several times a day.

He says that when I get back, she wants to throw us an

                    official engagement party.

You know, if this were a movie, that would mean I'm not coming back alive.

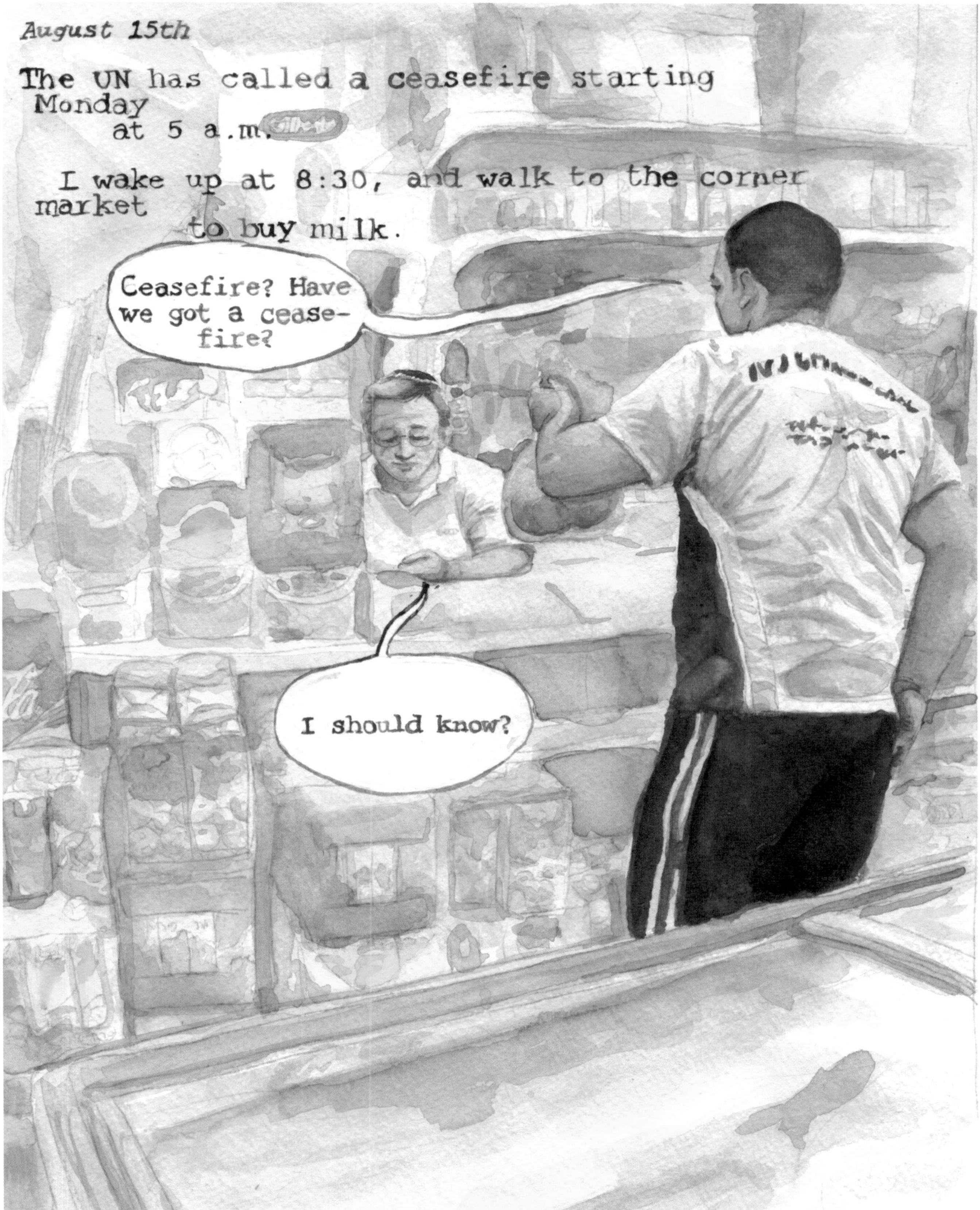
August 15th
The UN has called a ceasefire starting Monday at 5 a.m.
I wake up at 8:30, and walk to the corner market to buy milk.
Ceasefire? Have we got a cease-fire?
I should know?

Is it the end of the war? Did we win? Did they?

My mother sighs and says,
"I think it's the way most
                    wars in Israel have
           ended."

People I see are brimming with relief. Everyone
 I know has a
brother or a boyfriend
      serving reserve duty in Lebanon.

                    They'll all come home now.

August 17

I'm so glad it's over.
I'm glad for everyone's brothers and boyfriends. I'm glad I'll be coming back
home as the girl who saw her family, not as
the girl who's been
visiting a war.
I'd like to move in polite circles
without being the Israeli monster who laughs and
bombs
children.

Or at least,
I'm
bombing fewer
children than
before.

"The sons will
return to their
borders"
Jeremiah 31:16

Gilad Shalit and the rest of the
still-captured soldiers remain
postered
all over the country.

35

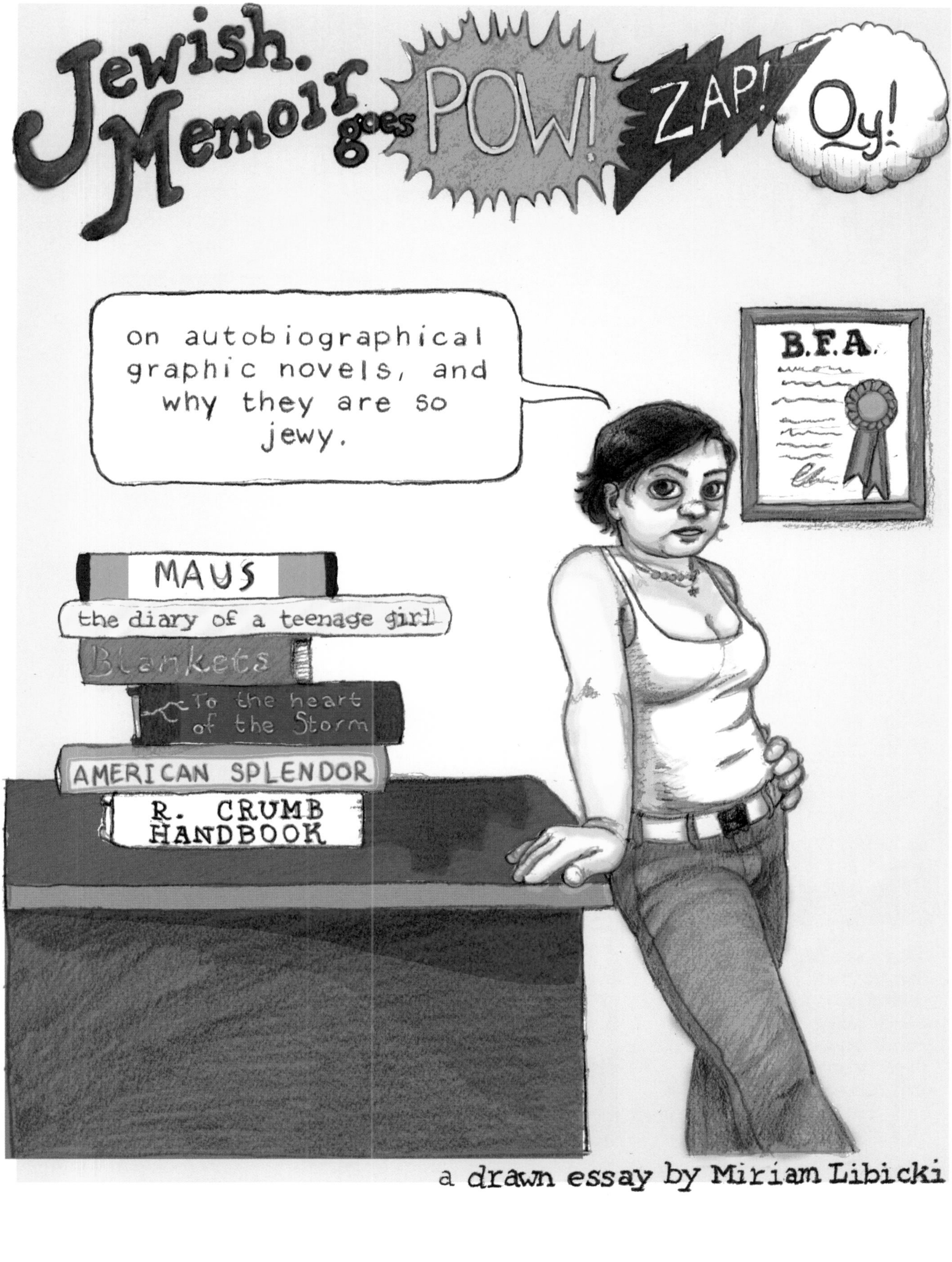
Jewish. Memoir goes POW! ZAP! Oy!
on autobiographical graphic novels, and why they are so jewy.
B.F.A.
MAUS
the diary of a teenage girl
Blankets
To the heart of the Storm
AMERICAN SPLENDOR
R. CRUMB HANDBOOK
a drawn essay by Miriam Libicki

Jewish Memoir goes POW! ZAP! Oy!

written, illustrated, and pilfered by Miriam Libicki

It is possible that the blueprints for the modern autobiographical comic have been hidden in Jewish tradition for millennia.

It is possible that Moshe Rabbeinu was the first autobiographer, and tradition tells us he was a reluctant one. Moshe, allegedly the humblest among men, altered one letter in the Bible G-d was dictating to him, making it smaller, to downplay an instance of G-d's intimacy with him.

Or if we see all of the Hebrew Bible as the Jews' collective autobiography, it is a remarkably raw and ambivalent one. How many people's national story puts both the people and its god in such an often unflattering light?

We miss the fleshpots of Egypt!

SHADDAP!!

(Christianity, on the other hand, seems to prefer its good guys very very good and its bad guys very very bad, and no one goes back and forth between the two.)

(Almost from the beginning of Christian iconography, they decided to tack these circles onto the heads of some people, just so we don't forget who the good guys are.)

1

This is all possible. But the genre I work in was almost certainly established more recently, by a handful of Jews and Jew-sympathizers.

I'll call my genre, for the sake of this essay, gonzo literary comics. The word *gonzo* (coined about late journalist Hunter S. Thompson in the 1960s, etc.) refers to a creation in which the identity and presence of the creator is inextricably involved, often extending as far as risking the life, limb, or reputation of said creator. *Literary*, because the discussed autobiographies and semi-autobiographies are not confessions for confession's sake, but aim to reach out to the larger cultural conversation about the human condition, using tools from literature and high art, as well as creating techniques unique to comicking.

And *comics* because most of my sources are in the medium of sequential art. Not *graphic novels*, because that term implies book-like binding, in which many of these works did not find their original form. Many were written before the first acknowledged graphic novel, in 1979. My own comics, as of this writing, have not known perfect binding.

Philip Roth's <u>Portnoy's Complaint</u>, published in 1969, set off a storm of controversy in the United States, but especially among Jews and the young, about what is "ok to say in public."

The characters are broadly drawn; Roth has called the central family a Jewish joke. All the characters are very Jewish, the language is riddled with as many Yiddishisms as profanities, and the protagonist is engaged in psychoanalysis, a quintessentially Jewish pursuit.

Despite these very ethnic elements, <u>Portnoy</u> was a best-seller. It was emblematic of an era of confessional art, of plumbing one's own messy psychology for material.

And the other pioneers of this style in various media, from Alan Ginsberg to Leonard Cohen to Woody Allen, were disproportionately Jewish.

Roth has insisted that <u>Portnoy</u> is not at all autobiographical. But its language of raw confession, its rueful yet over-the-top humor, and its conversational narration was the perfect canvas for the gonzo literary comics shortly to come.

2

In the late sixties, R. Crumb was already the star of the underground comix scene. He did this strip in *The East Village Other* the same year that Portnoy was published, titled "Projunior's Cum":

Strangely enough, this strip presaged exactly the new and controversial direction Crumb's art was to take.

Crumb is not a Jew. But his art was overwhelmingly influenced by members of the tribe, from Harvey Kurtzman to Aline Kominsky. And, apparently due to a devotion to the iconoclastic 1950s MAD Magazine, Yiddishisms are almost as frequent in Crumb's work as in Roth's.

Crumb gained popularity as a druggie artist, but always held himself aloof from flower children, and felt very skeptical about the universe-curing powers of free love and consciousness expansion.

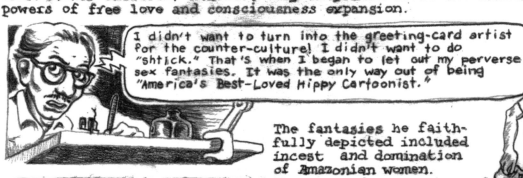

I didn't want to turn into the greeting-card artist for the counter-culture! I didn't want to do "shtick." That's when I began to let out my perverse sex fantasies. It was the only way out of being "America's Best-Loved Hippy Cartoonist."

The fantasies he faithfully depicted included incest and domination of Amazonian women. They were dangerous enough to make Crumb a pariah in certain circles for the next thirty years.

BROIGUL I AIN'T... LET'S FACE IT...

Yet by constantly pitting the id of his beautifully grotesque fantasies against the superego of enlightened (and his own) disapproval, he became the tortured, celebrated, art-world fixture he is today.

3

Another artist who borrowed a page from Philip Roth in order to forge the new and different genre in comics is Justin Green, in his 1972 underground work, Binky Brown Meets the Holy Virgin Mary.
Art Spiegelman calls it a major inspiration, and credits him with inventing the genre of "confessional autobiographical comix." Despite this, Green is virtually unknown to others than those interested in the history of comics.

Binky Brown follows its protagonist from childhood to young adulthood, as he is victimized by extreme Catholic guilt, puberty, and what we would now recognize as textbook, if severe, obsessive-compulsive disorder.

There is a Jewish element to Green's work, the title notwithstanding.

Green's (and his alter ego, "Binky's") father is Jewish, and his very existence makes the devoutly Catholic boy of Binky Brown feel like an outsider in his own community. Not through any action of his own, every time Binky's father appears in a panel that depicts Catholic ritual or theology, he spontaneously sprouts horns and a black Mickey Mouse-like nose.
Yet when Spiegelman says, "Justin turned comic book boxes into intimate secular confession booths,"
his language points to a distinction between American-Jewish style confessionalism and confessionalism undertaken from a (way the heck) Christian ethic/aesthetic. There are more gasps than laughs in Binky Brown. It sometimes seems like an unending litany of sins, much more like Catholic confession than Jewish storytelling. The preface assures us that the saga is....

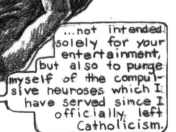

...not intended solely for your entertainment, but also to purge myself of the compulsive neuroses which I have served since I officially left Catholicism.

4

41

Harvey Pekar's *American Splendor* series also debuted in 1972, in an underground magazine called *The People's Comics*. As the periodical's name indicates, Pekar is a defiantly working-class writer, from a Marxist-Jewish family. Pekar was unique among underground cartoonists in that he was solely a writer and never an artist. Rather, he collaborated with several regular artists, most famously R. Crumb.

Their acquaintance was one of the great serendipitous moments in art/literary history, as Crumb gave distinctive, rumpled form to Pekar's rants and Pekar challenged Crumb to be more cerebral in his own work.

It was Pekar who, according to Crumb (and himself) first introduced literary realism into the genre. His stories are diaristic and observational. They avoid dramatic or decisive action, and often focus claustrophobically on the "Harvey" character going about his solitary business.

American Splendor is about Pekar's life as a file clerk scraping by in Cleveland. No psychedelic imagery, no shattering revelations of childhood trauma, and every character is life-size and no larger.

Pekar put out this honest, uncommercial work for decades before the literati were ready for him.

Now they say he's "a self laden with the techniques and inner-directed impulses of the most exacting of modern authors: self-pity and self-loathing, self-criticism and self-reference, self-consciousness above all" (Village Voice).

But postmodernism also constitutes an important element of Pekar's work. Because the character is drawn by multiple artists, with wildly divergent styles, the morphing features of "Harvey" consciously give the lie to "honesty" and "realism."

5

These four, more than any others, laid the groundwork for all the memoir comics to come.

Thirty-plus years later, artists, Jew and goy alike, from Art Spiegelman to Phoebe Gloeckner to Craig Thompson to me, trace our bodies overtop shadows of these funny, tragic, shamefaced, egotistical, wild-eyed, projectile-sweating, two-dimensional men.

6

I was not always the exaggerated line drawing you see before you. But comic books are practically my second language, and Hebrew is my third. I grew up in a very Jewish household, Shabbat, Kashrut, Orthodox synagogue and all.

We were the same ages as sibling supergroup Power Pack for awhile. I always suspected the Powers' father, a gentle, bearded scientist like mine, was Jewish.

But my parents were considered hippies in their community, and were remarkably open-minded with us kids. After my brother started collecting, I learned to read on Marvel comics.

I went to a private Jewish dayschool, so I never felt like an outsider due to my religion...

But I still knew my whole family were oddballs. None of my classmates read comic books, listened to Tom Lehrer or weren't allowed to bring friends home who didn't get along with all of their siblings. I read the Torah at my bat mitzvah, but opted out of the party. And even though we had money, we never had a television, let alone ski trips to Aspen.

As a kid, I certainly fit the creator-ly mold of shy, with occasional exhibitionism.

My best friend Frances and I had a game where we had discovered staring powder invisible to the naked eye but fearsome in its potency.

Sprinkle liberally.

Go into a crowd and do a spastic dance to activate...

And behold: stares!

My father was even a fan of R. Crumb, and Crumb was a titillating off-camera force of my childhood. My father would drag out the old comics from his college years, and crib Crumb's style for illustrations he did for synagogue fliers.

I saw the results, but the drawing all took place behind closed doors. By the time the doors opened, the R. Crumbs were hidden again, because they were not for children.

To this day I've never seen my father's Crumb comix. His great care in keeping them from us gave them such an ominous mystique that I couldn't bring myself to read Crumb until I was in college, even though I was in and out of comic shops all the time.

Cerebus and *Strangers in Paradise* were not for children either, so I hid them from my father.

My relationship with my local comic shop continued unabated until I left home, and only slightly abated after that.

In my early teens, I discovered "graphic novels" (Cerebus, *Strangers in Paradise*, the oeuvre of Will Eisner), and was pretty much done with superheroes.

I wasn't an aspiring comic artist, though; it seemed like tedious work, drawing the same things over and over. I was a draw-er of portraits during classtime, and self-portraits at home. I thought I'd be a children's book illustrator.

8

My first encounter with Philip Roth was in Israel, through a book of woodcuts by Moshe Hoffman, an Israeli contemporary of his.

It's probably why I don't have a problem thinking of Portnoy's Complaint as a comic book.

In the Israeli army, I kept a diary, but barely drew. Nevertheless, the mind-numbing uselessness of my army job made me ever more eager to go to university and be an art major.

In my first semester of art school, in practically my first week of real art school, a year after my discharge, and move back to North America, I drew the short story *rituk*. I didn't plan it that way, but it hit on many of the essential motifs of gonzo literary comics in its five pages.

then i felt bad for forgetting i was at a funeral

It is autobiographical, taken almost word-for-word from an army diary entry of mine. It is fairly miserable in tone, but contained its share of humor, which happened to be humor at the protagonist's expense. And it shows the protagonist failing at seduction, as she hits on her waiter and is ignored.

9

I'm not sure why I was initially taken with gonzo literary comicking, but I've learned that autobiography disguised as literature has advantages over straight autobiography, and straight literature.

P. Roth

We judge the author of a novel by how well he tells the story. But we judge morally the author of an autobiography, whose governing motive is primarily ethical as against aesthetic.

Gonzo literature is judged on aesthetics, but the way it draws directly on real life (and affects real life in turn) allows it to also explore one big ethical question:

Does being an artist mean you get to be a total selfish bastard, because your creative license just can't be fettered? Do your loved ones have to just like or lump being exposed in art? Does a talent for semi-autobiography give an artist a free opt-out of respecting others' wishes?

AMERICAN PASTORAL
Philip Roth

LEAVING A DOLL'S HOUSE
Claire Bloom

I MARRIED A COMMUNIST
Philip Roth

The 1990s Roth-Bloom feud

When I finished *rituk*, I posted it online. It wasn't long before I got an irate email from the ex I'd blithely mentioned by name in the story. I wasn't prepared for that.

But gonzo artists are gonzo artists because they just can't be nice. If we were nice and dutiful, our artwork would be lousy.

Rather than a memoir which may be read as narrowly concerning one life, a piece of gonzo literature can, through its use of fictional storytelling devices, be about as much as fiction can.

Stretching and changing the truth when it suits you, you can make an autobiographical story metaphorical, even universal. Comics often make use of surrealism and symbolism, which are much harder to pull off in autobiography told straight.

It is far from gonzo, but I keep thinking...

how much more valuable Madame Bovary is as fiction rather than a provincial Frenchwoman's autobiography.

MADAME BOVARY C'EST MOI

And if the character is an uglier you, and the story is sort of true, you get the credit for "honesty" and "bravery" as well.

MADAME BOVARY C'EST MOI

10

Comic books are even better at ambivalence than literature is.

What the comic book can do, which prose alone cannot, is to keep previous scenes physically before the reader after the narrative has moved on.

Joseph Witek (no picture available)

Not only can you literally show-don't-tell in comics, you can tell one thing while showing another.

When comics take on semi-autobiography, they are both more and less revealing than fictionalized autobiography.

More, because not only are you recording your most shameful moments, the moments are made graphic, in exaggerated drawings all over the page, where any kid in a comic shop can flip right to them.

But the stylized drawings of comic books are also an extra membrane of mediation between the creator and the reader's experience of her.

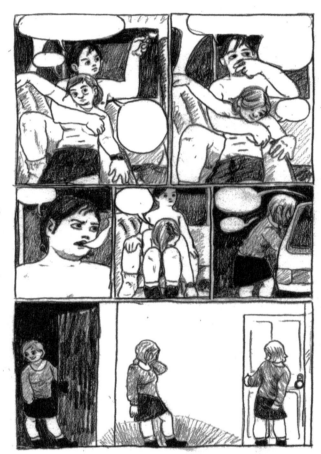

(This is not Miriam Libicki. You are unlikely to recognize Miriam Libicki on the street, with these drawings to go on.)

11

Comic style editorializes human appearance, fictionalizes it in order to bring certain aspects of humanity to light. The figure of the protagonist who is both "the author" and sometimes hard to have sympathy for is integral to gonzo literary comics. Basically the opposite of "the candidate you'd most like to have a beer with."

Comic Jason Green is a basket case.

Comic R. Crumb is a creepy misanthrope.

Comic Harvey Pekar is moody and judgmental, not to mention dingy in a different way for every artist who draws him.

And comic Miriam is passive and lumpish.

(on the upside, straight male readers may feel they have even-ish odds of going to bed with her...)

12

Jewish tradition is not lacking in less-than-perfect heroes. Jews interesting themselves in imperfection led to the whole enterprise of psychoanalysis, whose language and themes drive all Western autobiographical fiction.

Li'l Freud

I was ten or twelve years old, when my father began to take me with him on his walks. It was, on one such occasion, that he told me a story to show how much better things were now than they had been in his days ...

"When I was a young man," he said, "I went for a walk one Saturday in the streets of your birthplace; I was well dressed, and had a new fur cap on my head. A Christian came up to me and with a single blow knocked off my cap and shouted, 'Jew! Get off the pavement!'"

"And what did you do?" I asked.

"I went into the roadway and picked up my cap," was his quiet reply.

This struck me as unheroic conduct on the part of a big, strong man who was holding the little boy by the hand.

Human imperfection, imperfectability, collides with the Christian-influenced Enlightenment culture's assurance that perfection is not only desirable, but describable, and not only describable, but achievable. This is where outsiders come from.

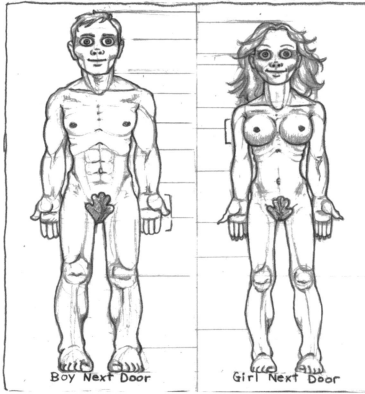

Boy Next Door

Girl Next Door

These figures (silicone implants notwithstanding) are growing increasingly skeletal. Perhaps they are moving away from Enlightenment materialism to a purer Christian spirit-body divide, where you live only to die as beautifully as you can.

Eunuch Next Door

13

Jewish outsiders like Ginsburg, Cohen, and Roth shocked the system by neither hiding nor striving to fix the imperfect parts of themselves. Self-obsessed? Have "issues"?

Get a *room*, the American phrase goes.

Well, the Jews practically never say that. We are a people without a room. The conspiracy of imagined purity has always been someone else's club. As outsiders, we don't benefit from it. As iconoclasts, we don't take it with a straight face.

And for two millennia the Jews haven't had a room, but no one's paying attention anyway. Then here comes Roth shouting, 'Hey, look at us! We don't have a room!'

Joel Rothschild, genzo songwriter

I'd like to meet him, but I wouldn't want to shake his hand!

Jacqueline Susann on Roth, on *The Tonight Show*

For god's sake don't inflict your tale of depravity and woe on innocent strangers. Not if there isn't some kind of salvation at the end of it.

14

The confessional Jews (and honorary Jews) dwell on the quirks and neuroses and damages of human characters, not because wretchedness or wickedness is aesthetically powerful in contrast to goodness, but because that's what's really real in life.

Once privacy and discretion are gotten rid of, certain motifs are repeated. Shame, and certain acts widely recognized as shameful, need to take place onscreen to establish the protagonist as both grimily human and trustworthy (at least as far as you can throw a graphic novel).

15

MASTURBATION was a mainstay for the founding fathers of gonzo literary comics.

It was not the first piece of liver I had defiled

Roth

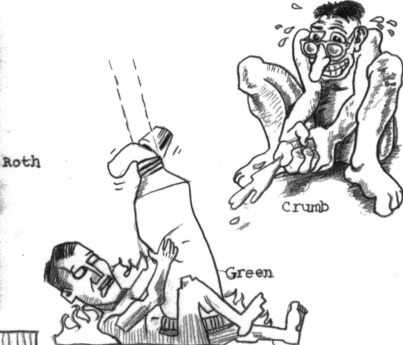

Crumb

Green

AHHH...

Pekar

Even my co-gener-ation-alist Craig Thompson.

No masturbation scenes in *jobnik!*, as yet.
But in the spirit of solidarity—

16

Also present is the acknowledgement, explicit or implied, that gonzo artists make their stories out of not just our own misery, but THE MISERY OF OTHERS. Those who are or were close to the author who get all the real-life misery but none of the literary rewards.

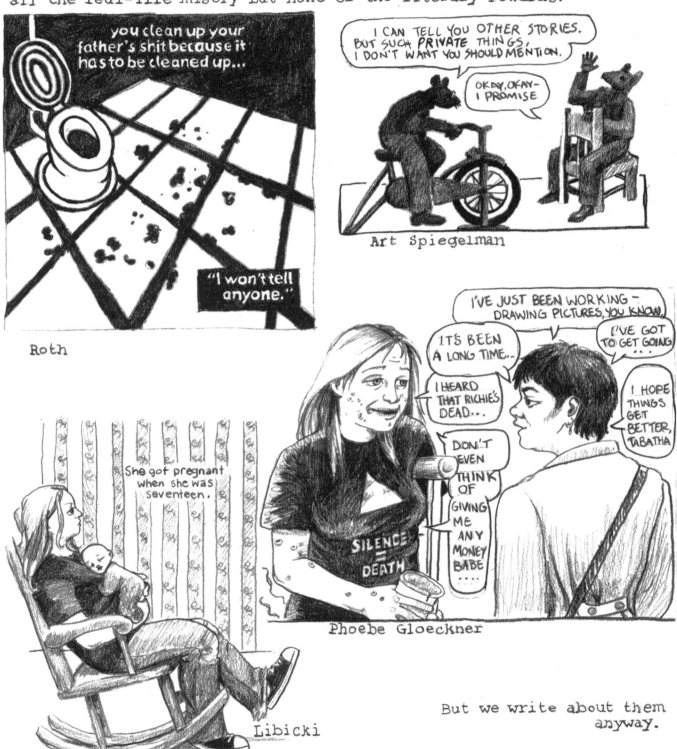

Roth

Art Spiegelman

Phoebe Gloeckner

Libicki

But we write about them anyway.

The third recurring shame is SHAME ITSELF. Shame which is misplaced, and becomes an actually destructive force; Shame you are ashamed to have felt.

Pekar

Will Eisner

For pre-baby boom artists, this shame often centers around immigrant fathers.

Justin Green's *oeuvre* contains many fine examples of the destructiveness of shame. In fact, it is impossible to excerpt one panel, when it is the unifying theme of all Green's work

Libicki

18

The differences between me, in my twenties and diving into the scene in 2005, and them, in their twenties and scratching out the scene in 1970, seem greater than the similarities.

I'm third-generation, meaning I don't have immigrant parents to embarrass me, or push me naïvely out into a world they can't ever understand. My childhood Judaism wasn't a ghetto Judaism suddenly lost without its ghetto. My parents grew up in American secularism, and chose Modern Orthodoxy in adulthood.

> NOW MA, SHH!

> DON'T SHUSH ME! IT'S TRUE...YOU'RE A GOOD BOY AND GOOD TO YOUR MOTHER....GOD WILL LOOK AFTER YOU FOR THAT... BELIEVE ME!!

I grew up in a religious environment designed to survive alongside secularism and consumer capitalism.

Jews are not the visible minority they once were. I never saw my father get his hat knocked off by a big goy, literally or metaphorically speaking.

I enjoyed masturbating from a very early age, but the most my parents ever said was

> Don't do that in the living room...

Probably why my masturbation hasn't made it into *jobnik!* I don't find the subject quite as fascinating as the old guys do.

19

But after the childhood of happy nerds, financial security and Judaism done right, I'm in Vancouver, while my parents and sister are in the Holy Land.

I'm writing morose comics that inspire concern in those close to me, and "shacking up," as I told the *Jewish Daily Forward*, "with a Buddhist."

Home.

I went to Israel, pledged my soul to it
...
and came back.

Still? even post *Orientalism* and intifada, when we know that Israel is the ultimate post-colonial/neo-colonial villain?

Israel is almost Western and almost a colonial power. Close enough, really.

Plus, there's this neat symmetry where Jews, the ultimate victims (Holocaust), are now the ultimate oppressors.

It makes great copy.

I write all about Israel, but they can't show my drawn essay at the local JCC because my "love for Israel is not evident," and I'd break the Holocaust survivors' hearts.

I live in a very non-Jewish town, with few Jewish friends, and feel Jewish, and want to be Jewish, more than I ever have before.

You may have noticed this piece, with all its masturbation scenes and phalluses, is hardly a Nice Jewish Essay. I tried...

20

Traditional fiction's aesthetics require the creator to lose her sense of self in order to access the universal human condition, and in non-fiction, including autobiography, we expect at least an attempt at dispassionate objectivity. In gonzo aesthetics, the deepest truth is found in hyper-self-consciousness, which is quite unlike traditional fictional aesthetics or non-fictional reportage.

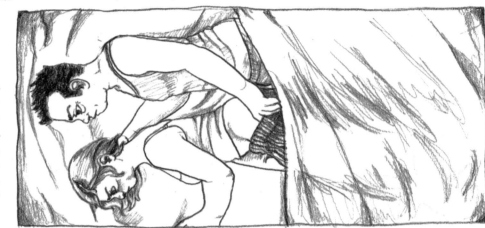

It also requires that you don't always like what you find, and that's a heck of a way to live.

Maybe it's best for a confessional artist to be

...one of those Jews, like Job, who wonder why they were born.

P. Roth

Being conflicted, being ashamed but not sure you're sorry, is a powerful way to get at truths.

I'm not sure, but I'm sure that nobody should be sure.

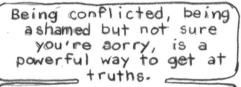

Being conflicted is the right thing to do until oh no, now I am doing the right thing and can't be conflicted!

oy, chevrelach!

shanda fur de goyim!

21

Bibliography and Graphic Sources

Cooper, Alan. Philip Roth and the Jews. New York: State University of New York Press, 1996.

Crumb, R., and Peter Poplaski. The R. Crumb Handbook. London: MQ Publications, 2005.

Eisner, Will. To the Heart of the Storm. New York: DC Comics, 1991.

Freud, Sigmund. The Interpretation of Dreams. Trans. James Strachey. New York: Basic Books, Inc., 1955.

Green, Justin. Binky Brown Sampler. San Francisco: Last Gasp, 1995.

Gloeckner, Phoebe. A Child's Life and Other Stories. Berkeley: Frog, 2000.
---. The Diary of a Teenage Girl : An Account in Words and Pictures. Berkeley: Frog, 2002.

Gordon, Andrew. "Jewish Fathers and Sons in Spiegelman's Maus and Roth's Patrimony." ImageTexT: Interdisciplinary Comics Studies. 1, no. 1 (2004). 5 Jan 2007.

Katz, Uri, ed. Moshe Hoffman Woodcuts, 1966-1980. Jerusalem: The Jerusalem Print Workshop and Friends, 1989.

Libicki, Charles. "1st Annual Latke-Hamentaschen Debate" cartoon.

Libicki, Miriam. Jobnik! 5 vols. Vancouver: Real Gone Girl, 2006. www.realgonegirl.com

Park, Ed. "Losing His Voice." The Village Voice. July 30 – August 5, 2003.

Pekar, Harvey, Kevin Brown, et al. American Splendor : The Life and Times of Harvey Pekar. New York : Ballantine Books, 2003.
Pekar, Harvey, Dean Haspiel, et al. The Quitter. New York : DC Comics, 2005.

Roth, Philip. Portnoy's Complaint. New York: Random House, 1969.
---. Reading Myself and Others. New York: Farrar, Straus & Giroux, 1975.
---. The Facts : A Novelist's Autobiography. New York: Farrar, Straus & Giroux, 1988.

Spiegelman, Art. Maus : A Survivor's Tale. New York: Pantheon Books, 1997.

Thompson, Craig. Blankets : An Illustrated Novel. Marietta: Top Shelf Productions, 2003.

Witek, Joseph. Comic Books as History : The Narrative Art of Jack Jackson, Art Spiegelman, and Harvey Pekar. Jackson : University Press of Mississippi, 1989.

fierce ease

Portraits of
Israel
August/September
2008

Ashkelon, August 26

I've come back to Israel almost two years, to the week since my visit at the end of the last Lebanon war, after which I wrote a watercolour essay presenting wartime Israel to North Americans.

It's beautiful but incredibly hot at my parents' place. On the way to the beach, I take a picture for my husband of a wild parrot in a palm tree.

Jerusalem, August 30
At my sister's place now, I'm feeling nostalgic.
From 1998-2002, Naomi was my family
and this was my town.

Ronnen, a good friend from those times, has come over to visit. I tell him I often wish I could move back. He looks at me weird.

Here?? Why? I'm thinking of leaving again. This country has just gone to shit since the last war.

What? What happened since the last war?

Everyone's so belligerent and no one's thinking logically.

The things that happen in a week can devastate you. It's like a background noise that doesn't let you eat or sleep or indulge... The living here is so intense, I can't really imagine staying here 'til I'm forty.

Tel Aviv, September 1

I'm suddenly ashamed that I didn't know that everything is different, that everything has gone to Hell since the last time I was here.

I was happy to be here to report on the end of a war, which was a short war and didn't seem terribly bad as far as deaths or destruction. I got my comic book out of it, and maybe I expected Israel to sit nicely until I got back.

When Lisa, a Canadian-Israeli reporter and a newer friend, mentions her pessimism, I seize the opportunity: are things much worse here now than they were two years ago?

Yes. Hezbollah is stronger, more popular, and better positioned than before.

But even more than that, everyone just feels hopeless. The oligarchs have taken over. A half-dozen families control the major media, papers, and TV.

Here's a recent story. An investigative journalist, Miki Rosenthal, made a documentary on the Ofers, one of the most prominent families in Israel, on how they made their money and what they do with it, and had a deal to show it on the YES network. The Ofer family threatened a lawsuit and YES dropped the documentary, no other network would touch it, even the old national one.

The Israeli journalists' union called an "emergency meeting," and all the old socialist-Zionist journalists who make NIS1000 a month came out and pumped their fists... Only one guy there stood up and said "we all know the rich families own the media, and it's forbidden to do any investigative journalism about them. Beforehand nobody spoke up, and now, nobody's in a position to do anything about it. When the dust settles, you'll never work in journalism again. Nice that you tried to stick your neck out, but brother, you've eaten it."

I moved **back** to Israel in 2000, right before the intifada. And I am more pessimistic now than then, even though things on the face may look better for Israelis. It's been very hard the past two years after the war, especially with my trip to Lebanon 13 months ago. Like a lot of Israelis, I'm just emotionally exhausted. You see so much stupidity and avarice and megalomania, in such a small country, and you just can't be optimistic anymore. I resent that I seem to have lost my belief in the possibility of change.

I'm definitely looking for a backup plan, to Israel. I love it here, but I don't see anyone taking care of it. I'm very worried about the future of this country. Five years ago, I would have been horrified to be thinking of an escape, a "plan b."

I've had more opportunity to be a journalist since 2002. I've interviewed top politicians, army officers, settler leaders, Palestinian leaders... I'm aware of the complexities here, but looking at the way the PA is run, the way the Knesset is run, the prime minister's office — my God, what a cesspool.

It's both that I see more than I've ever seen, but also the apathy of Israelis allows this to happen. 70% of Israelis will say they oppose the occupation, but they send their sons to serve in the occupation, and nothing can get better.

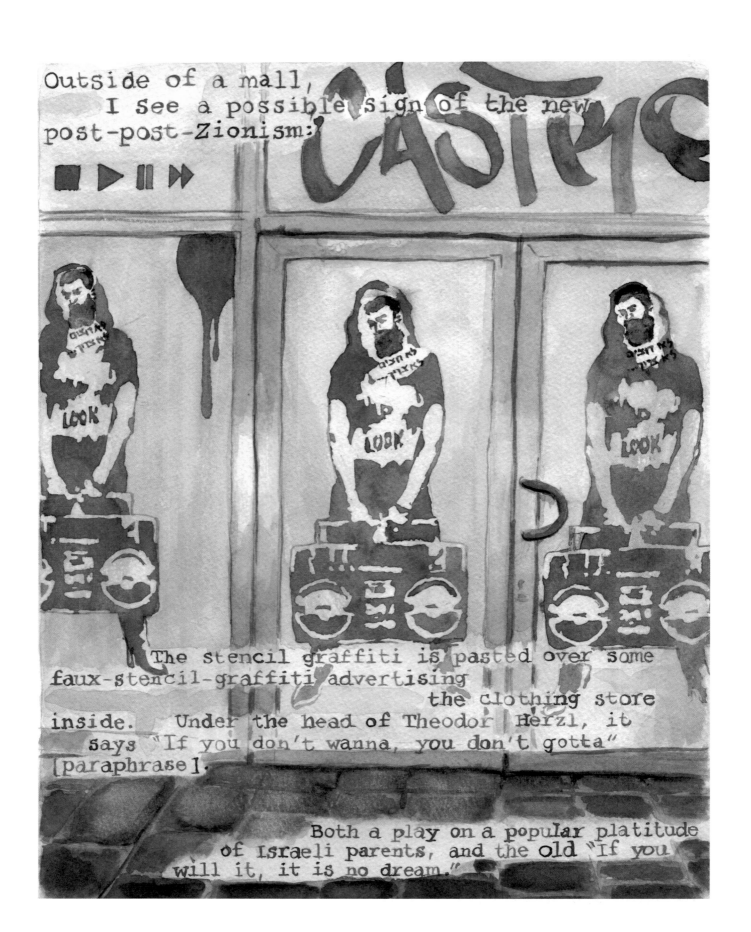

Outside of a mall,
    I see a possible sign of the new
post-post-Zionism:

The stencil graffiti is pasted over some
faux-stencil-graffiti advertising
                    the clothing store
inside.   Under the head of Theodor Herzl, it
    says "If you don't wanna, you don't gotta"
[paraphrase].

                Both a play on a popular platitude
        of Israeli parents, and the old "If you
    will it, it is no dream."

The papers seem to support Lisa's conclusion.

There's an ugly bribery scandal attached
to the prime minister. There's enough weight to
the charges that Olmert has been forced to
resign,   though he won't say
when he's leaving.

People I know are unshocked, medium-
outraged,   and sure that anyone with a
              chance of being elected will be
worse for the country.

המשטרה בהמלצה חמורה ביותר:
שוחד

The beginning of Olmert's front-page
              troubles can be traced to the end of the
war, when reservists called it a disaster,
              and blamed him.

During the war,   all eyes were upon Israel as it
       apparently plunged the middle east into the beginnings
of World War III, but visiting, life here seemed
                          its usual abnormal-normal.
In the meantime, the world has moved on
       as if the small summer war never happened, while Israeli
              society is quaking from the impact.

While I'm here, I should put
on my comics-journalist hat and get to the
bottom of
       this.

Jerusalem, September 8

I went back to Ronnen, to expand on what he'd said, now that I have a story.

Israel itself doesn't know where its priorities are, where it wants to go. The war was very dramatic, in that people felt betrayed by the generals, but I think it's just nostalgia for the glorious victories of the past.

Israel is a post-traumatic state, and the public opinion is always hysterical. That's since forever. And we're still in the middle east, we're not in Europe. It can get better or it can get worse, but I don't think it will be tragical or devastating. The casualties still represent a low-medium conflict.

My wife gets depressed when I talk like this. She's like, "Ok, let's go." We both think there's no chance for peace in the short term.

We did half a year in New Zealand, four months in Australia, and four months in Holland, but it's hard to imagine living in another place as a permanent resident. I can get through the language barrier, the culture barrier, but I get homesick really easily.

I don't think Israel is a lion's mouth. I don't have, like, existential fear. I'm a foreign relations student, I've learned that nothing is unique, nothing is... singular. There's fundamentalists and corruption fighting democracy all over. It's kind of comforting to think, actually.

It's kind of a love-hate thing. When I'm here, I hate it. When I'm there... well, I hate it too. But it's my place, you know.

Yehuda Amichai had the poem, you know, "I want to die in my own bed"? he wrote it after the '48 war. One line goes, "you'll learn that you can furnish a lion's mouth."

68

Haifa, September 10

I traveled to the formerly besieged north, too dangerous for me to visit last trip, to see if the answers were clearer. Adi is an old army buddy. She lived in Tel Aviv during the war, but moved to Haifa immediately afterward. I ask her about what I've missed since the war.

In the last two years... I think we know who we as Israel are dealing with, how much Hezbollah and the Lebanese hate us, and what they are willing to do, kidnap soldiers....

Sometimes I have dreams about sirens, and going down to a bomb shelter and the end of the world, but I don't know if it's about the past Lebanon war, or just the coexistence in general,

All the Haifa'im I talk to just say it made them more connected to their home. I think anywhere else in Israel they would have just fallen apart. Haifa is like its own country, the people are wiser and tougher...We have the water and the mountains, and what else do we need?

I'd really like to ask some Arabs here what it was like for them. I know they had to go down to their bomb shelters too... The building where I live now has a bomb shelter, and it's mostly Arab, but I know there are a few elderly Jews. I wonder how they called everyone down to the bomb shelter, and what they talked about while they were there.

Haifa, September 11
Ruti is a family friend and Haifa resident.

I remember I came to this park during the war — I couldn't stay in the house any longer, I was going crazy up there. But this place was completely empty, deserted.

I think everything has returned totally to normal, everyone's forgotten about the war. Sometimes people talk about it, but, you know.

It's funny, but the one thing that's come out of it is I have friends in my building now. And it's from all those days we spent in the bomb shelter together, and we had to talk to pass the time. Before that — who meets all the neighbours in their apartment complex these days? But now I know them, and it's more than just saying "hi" in the stairwell.

Well, the other thing is that now when I hear a motorcycle going by, and it starts sounding like a missile, or there's a plane overhead — my heart just stops. I have goosebumps even talking about it. Like, you won't be thinking about it, then something happens, and you're right back there. But, you know. We don't have some great trauma, thank God.

70

Vancouver September 15

So I go back to Canada to sit down and write my book. But what can I tell the North Americans? Have I or haven't I witnessed some great trauma?

The only conclusion I have is that no matter how I try to relate to Israel — tourist, former resident, or journalist — I'm mostly an outsider who can't really understand.

And I don't know when I'll go back to the old lion's mouth, nation like any other nation.

strangers

A long-distance
view of Israel
May/June 2012

All sans-serif text is quotes or excerpts (further edited for length) from internet sources gathered between 24 May and 21 June 2012.

Text in red is from YNet: www.ynetnews.com

Text in blue is from National Public Radio online: www.npr.org

Text in orange is from the Hebrew Immigrant Aid Society: www.hias.org

Text in purple is from The Forward online: www.forward.com

Text in green is from the New York Times online: www.nytimes.com

Text in brown is from the Hotline for Migrant Workers' twitter feed: @HMWIsrael

Text in yellow is from Jewschool: www.jewschool.com

Lisa Goldman (@lisang) is a journalist who writes for 972 online magazine, among others.

Ben Murane (@kungfujew18) is the Director of New Generations New York at New Israel Fund

I tweet as @realgonegirl but it's mostly baby pictures right now.

disclaimers:
the art is meant as illustration, and does not necessarily correspond to the dates or the articles it appears alongside.
when I quote Hebrew facebook posts, the translation is my own, & should not be read as my friends' words, but the impressions that emerged after passing through my rusty Hebrew comprehension.

thanks to all the Israelis, for most of the text, & to Mike Yoshioka for half of the lettering.

For Mered Y.

Tel Aviv, September 2008

When I was in Israel back in 2008, I told my friend Lisa, who's a reporter, that I wanted to do a comics essay about the Ethiopian-Israelis.

Nah,

she said.

The real story is about the Sudanese in Israel, the refugees. You should write about them.

Coquitlam, May 24 2012   Haven't written my Ethiopian-Israeli
essay yet,   I spent a few
    months researching, then stalled   out. Home with my first
                                baby now, she's a couple
                                   weeks old.

        And suddenly the
     story is unquestion-
     ably about   the
       Sudanese Refugees.

Clashes erupt during south TA protest, migrants attacked
Residents say streets 'no longer safe'due to influx of African infiltrators
MK Regev: They are a cancer in our society

                                        About 1,000 people gathered in
                                      South Tel Aviv's Hatikva neighborhood
                                      to protest against the government's
                                         handling of the flow of African
                                            migrants into Israel.
                                         Some of the demonstrators
                                         shattered the windshield of a
                                         vehicle in which three African
                                            migrants were riding.

                        Smaller protests against the illegal immigration
                    phenomenon were held in Bnei Brak, Ashdod, Ashkelon and Eilat.
                Residents of the south Tel Aviv neighborhoods Shapira and Kiryat Shalom
              held another rally on Chahmei Yisrael Street. They waved signs reading, "Our
                  streets are no longer safe for our children," "The craziness of our life:
              Neglect, crime, rape and violence," "Yesterday it was my daughter, tomorrow
                        it will be your daughter," and "Yishai was right".

Tel Aviv, September 2008

So what is the story? האילונטיי הבניעי

what was the story in 2008, and
what is the story now?

MAGEN DAVID IN ISRAEL

מגן דוד אדום בישראל

ריאות הפליטים

Five years ago, when the number of Africans in Israel was in the hundreds, rather than the thousands, the Jewish state's policies toward the group were touted as an example to other nations.
At the time, Israeli soldiers and civilians talked about the need to help African refugees. The wife of then Prime Minister Ehud Olmert spoke of getting personally involved.

That's my memory. That it was a credit to Israel, being the only democratic country with a land border with Africa, that these refugees were walking thousands of miles to get here, and being welcomed.

CALL SUDAN
1122
1084
CALL AFRICA
1116
1116
BEGE CALL SUDAN
1085
NIGERIAN LEOPARD
1124
05
TO SUDAN

In 2008, I went back home and ___ didn't take Lisa's advice. But I took a few photos at the bus station in South Tel Aviv, that seemed to be signs of the times refugees at an official clinic inside the station and a kiosk display which suggested some refugees could and did call home.

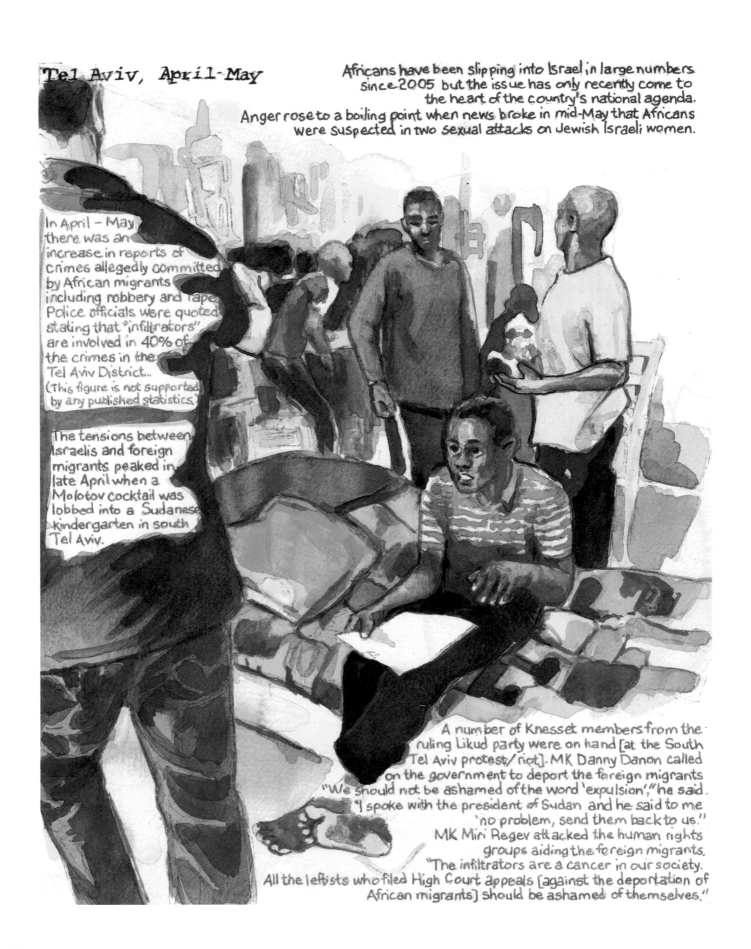

Tel Aviv, April-May

Africans have been slipping into Israel in large numbers since 2005 but the issue has only recently come to the heart of the country's national agenda. Anger rose to a boiling point when news broke in mid-May that Africans were suspected in two sexual attacks on Jewish Israeli women.

In April – May there was an increase in reports of crimes allegedly committed by African migrants, including robbery and rape. Police officials were quoted stating that "infiltrators" are involved in 40% of the crimes in the Tel Aviv District. (This figure is not supported by any published statistics.)

The tensions between Israelis and foreign migrants peaked in late April when a Molotov cocktail was lobbed into a Sudanese kindergarten in south Tel Aviv.

A number of Knesset members from the ruling Likud party were on hand [at the South Tel Aviv protest/riot]. MK Danny Danon called on the government to deport the foreign migrants. "We should not be ashamed of the word 'expulsion'," he said. "I spoke with the president of Sudan and he said to me 'no problem, send them back to us.'" MK Miri Regev attacked the human rights groups aiding the foreign migrants. "The infiltrators are a cancer in our society. All the leftists who filed High Court appeals [against the deportation of African migrants] should be ashamed of themselves."

Tel Aviv, May

A week after the first protest/riot in South Tel Aviv there is another.

The anti-migrant protesters included well-known right-wing activists Baruch Marzel and Itamar Ben-Gvir. Participants held up signs urging a fair share in responsibility for the migrant population specifically that they be housed in economically advantaged north Tel Aviv as well. "This is South Tel Aviv, not South Sudan," one poster read.

Five protesters were arrested for rioting and another was detained on suspicion of incitement.

The protesters were thrown a curve ball when an Israeli of Ethiopian descent named Hananiya passed by. The demonstrators, mistaking him for a migrant, began to swear at him and hit him. "These people are crazy," Hananiya told Ynet. "I came by because I was interested in the protest, and got hit. At work they joke that I can't walk around here, and it's true. This is what racism is," he said.

79

After that, every other day seems to bring a new outbreak of racist violence.

A group of 11 teens from Tel Aviv (all aged 14-18) has been charged with attacking Sudanese and Eritrean migrants in "revenge" attacks. The indictment states that 10 of the group are accused of "racially motivated" attacks in which the teens would attack foreigners who crossed their path, using boards and pipes. In two cases, they stole the plaintiffs' bicycles. A teenage girl is accused of property crimes but not of assault.

Abdullah Abuya, 40, from Darfur, is lying beaten and injured in his house in Eilat, after he was allegedly attacked by seven guests at the Club Hotel where he works. One hotel guest described the incident on her Facebook page, writing: "We almost witnessed a lynch. Seven intoxicated guys decided to lynch a Sudanese housekeeper. He could have been thrown from the fifth floor window, or die from punches and kicks to his head. This was happening a few centimeters from us."

Magen David Adom emergency services received a report at 4 am on Saturday about an unconscious Sudanese man on Sderot Har Zion Street in South Tel Aviv. A medical team that arrived at the scene found the man with injuries all over his body. Police investigators collected testimonies from eyewitnesses, and shortly afterwards arrested a suspect.

On Sunday, a video depicting an Israeli man hurling a raw egg on an African migrant was uploaded to the web. The police department is attempting to determine the identity of the web user who uploaded the video.

A Jerusalem apartment housing foreign workers was torched overnight. Firefighters rescued 10 people, four of whom needed medical attention. The Fire Department said that their investigation indicated arson. Investigators also found the words "Get out of the neighborhood" sprayed on one of the walls.

Coquitlam, May 31   I am horrified, but not too   horrified to
                        remember I have a big convention coming up, and no
new comics, nothing to show for myself except, of course, the baby.

        But I've been doing all this research about tensions
    around
        Jewishness and Blackness! And Lisa prophesied this four years
ago! This has to be what my next drawn essay is about.

I hear on facebook about a   counter-demonstration planned in
    Tel Aviv, and try to delegate friends in Israel to be my eyes and
        ears there, if I'm getting all the news long-   distance, I
            can do a journalistic piece the same way.

facebook

Janice Fernheimer
May 31 at 1:44am ·

unfortunately, we won't be in TLV for this event this weekend, but I thought some of you
who will be might be interested in this event (English follows Hebrew)!

יומכם ואת יוזמתו עצרת יעברו עמכ! African Solidarity Party
Saturday, June 2 at 3:00am at כיכר רבין

Like · Comment · Unfollow Post · Share   1

👍 Rachel C_____ likes this.

Miriam Libicki oh, that's too bad, i was thinking of doing an emergency painted essay on this
business, but I'd need to delegate (/collaborate) with someone who can be there & take pictures &
impressions. hmm, Ranen Omer-Sherman, are you going to this maybe?
May 31 at 2:34am · Like

facebook

Miriam Libicki
May 31

any of my israeli peoples going to this & want to take pictures/notes for a possible essay of mine? Ronen S____
Micka R___ Shaul F_____, anybody?

סטטוס! ייבת עצרת סולידריות עם הפליטים האפריקאים! African Solidarity Party
Saturday June 2 at 3:00am at כיכר רבין ג'ויג

Like · Comment · Share

👍 Fred N_____ likes this.

Micka R_____ Thanks for sharing this I didn't know about it, but know that I do, I actually might be going. I
won't be taking notes or photos, but don't mind telling you about it later. Convince Ronen & Anat to tag along.

June 2

My friends are game,
but the results are

anti-climactic.

solidarity gathering   ▭   Inbox X

Omer-Sherman, Ranen ~~ranensherman@miami.edu~~   Jun 2 ☆
to me ▽

In the end, it was a very, very modest event. Just people gathering, no speakers or activities. At least
when I was there in the middle of the afternoon (it was supposed to conclude by 6:00).

I feel more impotent and further away
by the minute.

June I don't just feel far away physically, I start feeling
like I don't
    recognize this country anymore, or the people in it.

                I get most of my news from the twitter feeds
of my friends Ben,
        and Lisa. Ben is an American who's spent time living in
    Israel here and there, and works for Jewish nonprofits.

    Lisa is Canadian-born, spent half her life in Israel, but fled
the craziness back to Canada, like me. Maybe, try as we might, none
of us are really in touch with who "normal Israelis" are anymore.

According to a poll conducted by Tel Aviv University and the Israel Democracy Institute, 85% of Israeli Jews support the anti-African demonstrations. One-third identified with those protesters who turned violent toward them. More than half endorse the statement of Likud lawmaker Mini Regev that they are a "cancer" in the body of the nation.

Eilat Police spokesman Chief Insp. Lior Ben-Simon stated [about the two 24-year old suspects detained after the brutal beating of a Sudanese hotel worker] "These are normative people who were not intoxicated and do not have a criminal record."

Jerusalem, 1999

When I lived in Israel, I thought regular Israelis were, well, regular.

The Israelis I learned with in mechina (pre-army gap year program) my first year in the country were respectably liberal by-and-large. The mechina was dedicated to religious-secular tolerance, founded in the wake of the Rabin assassination. The mix of teenage cynicism and idealism of the kibbutznik kids inspired me to apply for Israeli citizenship.

In the army I served with a decidedly more mixed crowd, politically, economically racially... Americans ask me if I witnessed racism or anti-Arab sentiment in the army, but I'm hard-pressed to remember any.

I may have been too naïve to notice it, though.

June 1

Mechinistas are the Israelis I've stayed most in touch with. After I tag some in my post, a discussion arises in comments.

Miriam Libicki
May 31 at 2:25am · ✆

any of my israeli peoples going to this? was mine? Ronen S████, Micka R████, Shaul F████

African Soli
Saturday, June 2 at 3:00am at

Like · Comment · Unfollow Post · Share

👍 Fred N████ likes this

Micka R████ Thanks for sharing this! I didn't going. I won't be taking notes or photos, but I'm not tagging along, and you've got yourself a
May 31 at 3:33am · Like

Shaul F████ הנצבורית ומיקה - אם יש כסף לכתחנס...
[Hebrew text]
See More
May 31 at 4:25am · Like

Micka R████ [Hebrew text]
See More
May31 at 5:35am · Like 👍1

Shaul F████ The guess about Kristallnacht is wrong, the rest need a more detailed answer.
May 31 at 5:43am · Like

Shaul F████ [Hebrew text]
http://goo.gl/SyAcd
http://goo.gl/SyAcd
www.nrg.co.il
June 1 at 2:38am · Like · Remove Preview

Miriam Libicki Shaul F████, all perspective D████ Ronen S████ do it! i love to put
June 1 at 8:06pm · Like 👍1

Ronen S████ [Hebrew text paragraph]
June 2 at 2:49pm · Like

Shaul:
My English is fucked up, and this is an emotional subject, and I'm at work. I have a lot of solidarity for Africa, but this country can't absorb all of Africa into itself. We have to determine how to return the job-seekers as soon as possible. We have to keep refugees here for the moment, but we should not let them immigrate. Trying to absorb Africa into Israel has brought about the explosion of the inner cities. Leftist organizers here know how to tailor their messages to outside groups, who come dance here, or demonstrate here, but day-to-day they don't live here.

Micka:
I agree that the main protest should be against the current administration, to implement a humane solution for the refugees that does not come at the expense of other deprived populations. I understand inner city residents feel their meager turf threatened, but it's also fomenting xenophobia. I'd guess the Germans smashing windows on Kristallnacht were also underprivileged. Also, I love hearing about how I don't have the right to protest because I "don't live there." Even though, by the grace of God, I'm socio-economically privileged (well, as you know, more socio, less economic), every place I've lived since age 18 could be called an underprivileged neighborhood. On my street, there are foreign workers, Russians, Arabs, and Ashkenazi and Sephardi students. I'm sick of apologizing.

Ronen:
South Tel Aviv has been deteriorating since the '70s, from working-class neighborhoods into cauldrons of urban crime. Places like this are prone to violence of one sort or another. There are struggles against perceived "infiltrators" in communities across the country (Ramat Aviv Gimmel vs. the Chabad House, Kiryat Yovel vs. the ultra-orthodox, Kiryat Malachi vs. the Ethiopians), but minus this kind of violence. Most of the incitement came from the organized far-right, though the resident population is not far-right (witness the "Black Panthers") Which is to say that there's a surprising meeting of interests between opposite sides of the political spectrum, squeezing the statist, bourgeois center of the country.

There's an interesting connection between the events that instigated this storm. There were two incidents of rape in Tel Aviv, one by a Palestinian, the other by a group of asylum seekers. In both cases, the male partner of the victim was present, and urged her not to fight. In my opinion, this is an important point, because of the emphasis in all the inciting speeches about the rape of Jewish women by infiltrators as a deliberate practice. Not just the woman's honor was ruined, but her boyfriend's as well, recalling the archetypical "weak Jew." The feeling of Jewish victimhood seizes on the lack of resistance given, or the inability to meet violence with violence. Zionism and the Jewish settlement in Israel were founded by Jews fleeing from eastern Europe precisely because they could not defend against violence towards their communities.

Jerusalem, May-June So is it just a case of opportunists stoking flames easily stoked? The right-wing government stirring up populist sentiment to distract from the fact that they do nothing to relieve the worsening poverty in South Tel Aviv?

It is striking that so much of the evil words and policies come from two guys: Prime Minister Bibi Netanyahu, head of the "center-right" Likud, and Interior Minister Eli Yishai, head of the Ultra-Orthodox Shas. Both parties are historically popular among poor Sephardi Israelis, without actually helping them economically.

Yishai has been the most prolific, declaring that the majority of illegals are "criminals" and that they are responsible for raping Israeli women and infecting them with HIV. Yishai provided no evidence of either claim.

Yishai, whose own family immigrated to Israel from Tunisia, told the daily newspaper Maariv "Most of the people arriving here are Muslims who think the country doesn't belong to us, the white man."

The minister said that if given the mandate, there will not be a single infiltrator left in Israel in one year's time. "I would change the law so that every infiltrator is put in jail. Then he can decide whether he wants to remain imprisoned or go back to his home country."

Netanyahu contends that most of them are economic immigrants and that they threaten the Jewish character of Israel. On Sunday, he said that all new arrivals would immediately be placed in detention.

Before the wave of anger, the government was already building the world's largest detention facility, which will mean that Israel has room to detain 15,000 potential immigrants. A new law permits detaining all illegals for up to three years and some indefinitely.

June 7, the government wins a case allowing them to deport all South Sudanese. Days later, immigration police has arrested over 140 South Sudanese nationals before the expiration of the 1-week period granted to allow the asylum seekers to put their affairs in order. Most of those arrested are released after they sign a paper declaring that they are willingly returning to South Sudan. Those who sign are allowed to return home, collect their things, cash their paychecks and await the Ministry of Interior flights to Juba. Those who are not released are transferred to Saharonim and Giv'on prisons for migrants.

Tel Aviv, June

If it is just cynical populism (with potentially deadly effects), some in Israel are wise to it, even among inner-city South TelAvivians.

Shula Keshet, a resident of Neveh Sha'anan, added that it was important to her to take part in the protest to ensure that it didn't devolve into violence against Africans, no matter what country they were from.

"Violence against the refugees isn't acceptable – not as far as I'm concerned and not for many other residents. Our protest is against the policies of the government and the city and against the apartheid in Tel Aviv and the ghettos of poverty it creates. It's also racism that not a single refugee or infiltrator is sent to north Tel Aviv, just here."

Some Israelis invoke the biblical injunction to "love the stranger for we were strangers in the land of Egypt." Others say they now feel like strangers in their own country.

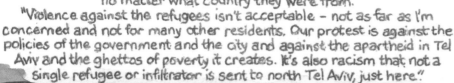

Inside the government there is embarrassment over the impression that mass deportations are imminent, and from the provocative statements of Minister Yishai.

"We're very frustrated by the Minister of the Interior and his populist statements," a senior Foreign Ministry source told the Forward. "Some of them are very irresponsible and they are causing great damage to Israel abroad."

Even regular Israelis see the horrifying irony in the "racial purification" Yishai and others seem to call for: "I feel I am in a movie in Germany, circa 1933 or 1936," said Orly Feldheim, 46, a daughter of Holocaust survivors, as she doled out food to a long line of immigrants in the neighborhood's Levinsky Park.

Tel Aviv, June   So is the globalized outrage and the bad press having an effect? Is it really any use?

My friend Janice, an American professor in Israel for the season shares some literal signs of the times.

Posters protesting the deportations of African refugees, they say at the bottom "I'm not an infiltrator, I'm a refugee." with testimonies of each.

Ben shares links constantly, and writes a long blog post exploring a report on Israel's asylum-granting (or asylum-denying) process. He says: My purpose is not fomenting popular disgust with the State of Israel But what are we all supposed to do with this information now?

Let me lend a historical comparison. A few years ago, investigative reports revealed the Jewish state had become a hub of the sex slave trade. The US State Department nearly dropped Israel from its list of good countries. Israel quickly implemented long-standing recommendations advised by Israeli human rights NGOs. Israel's role in the slave trade decreased and thus recovered its good name. It is civil society in Israel and internationally – including online communities like ours – who must play central roles in salvaging the Jewish people's sacred values from politicians unwilling to do so.

If you've not already signed Dan Sieradski's petition to Prime Minister Benyamin Netanyahu calling for the inciters to be fired, the process revamped, and asylum granted please do so now.

is that my role?

88

Coquitlam, June 21.

Israel is a big part of my identity. All my comics are about it. Many of my t-shirts But it's a part of my identity I feel I have to consciously maintain.

It takes effort to read my friends' Hebrew status updates. I've only been back once since 2008.

I left a life of luxury in Israel for a life of even more luxury in Canada. My Israeli passport is burning a hole in my purse These "infiltrators" walked half a continent for the privilege of living in a dirty city, taking under-the-table jobs if they find jobs at all, sending their children to schools upstanding citizens sometimes throw molotov cocktails through. But some have lived there eight years, and now they hang up posters to try to convince the citizenry to let them stay.

Who's the Israeli here? who is the stranger?

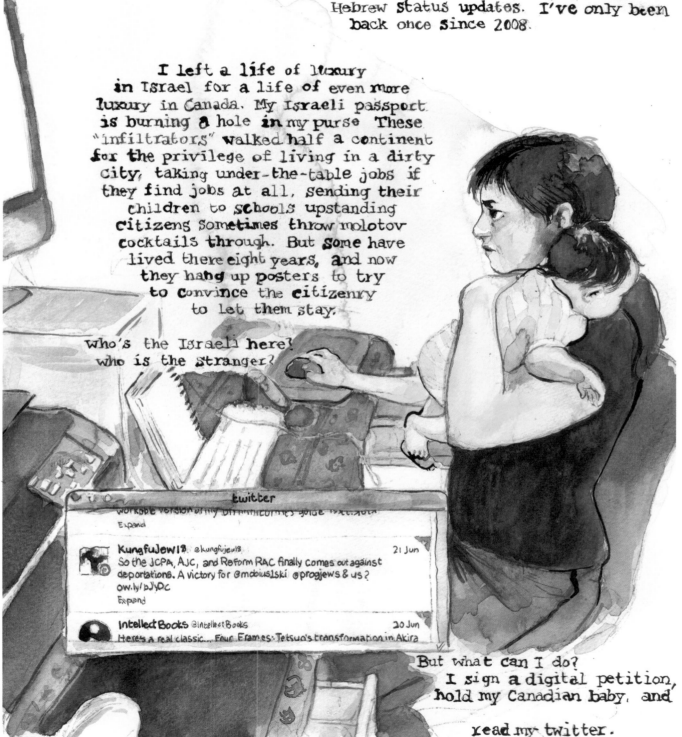

twitter

workable version of my birthcomics guide is at...out.
Expand

KungfuJew18 @kungfujew18   21 Jun
So the JCPA, AJC, and Reform RAC finally comes out against
deportations. A victory for @mobius1ski @progjews & us?
ow.ly/bJyDc
Expand

Intellect Books @Intellect Books   20 Jun
Here's a real classic... Four Frames: Tetsuo's transformation in Akira

But what can I do? I sign a digital petition, hold my Canadian baby, and

read my twitter.

Stranging the Welcomer

a theory of black and white
and jews all over

Part I: the Jews' Blacks

I met Sarah during basic training.

You go pray during breakfast, right? You're religious?

Yeah.

I went to a religious school, a boarding school. They gave all the Ethiopians a special entrance exam, though. It was all like Israeli history and European Jewish law and kibbutz crap... My parents don't even speak Hebrew!

We lived in the mountains! How was I supposed to know any of that stuff? So based on the test they decided I'm retarded. I couldn't even learn in the regular school, I was in a class that was all Ethiopians, and the worst rabbis. We had to take all these Judaism classes, even though my parents are strict religious! But they said our traditions were all wrong and weren't Torah.

They named me Sarah, which I think is completely ugly, so I would have a "real" fucking Jewish name. My real is Si___, though. It means 'gift.'

You could say I didn't know what to make of her.

I knew there were Ethiopian Israelis, of course, but I had no idea about the schools and the systemic racism.

The main emotion her story inspired in me was **guilt**, which is weird, because I didn't discriminate against her, and I'd been living in Israel 1/9th as long as she had, and what with my mother being a convert, I may have been more distantly related to the Israelis who mistreated her than she was.

But soon after this conversation, I really started noticing how shittily Ethiopian Israelis were treated and the patterns that shit fell into...

My close friends were soldier-teachers in the poor, overwhelmingly Mizrahi* neighbourhood where we had spent our gap year, and one of their unit was Ethiopian.

teacher! teacher!

hey soldier!

*Jews of Mid-Eastern/ North African descent

get outta here, kushi!*

hee hee hee

*nigger

Back at my base, watching a trashy soap set in a women's prison:

you bitch, you narced on me!

get her, Rachel!!

that's for putting the moves on my man, Svetlana!

kushi sambo!!

I started to feel more and more pissed off.

"Kushi" is bad enough, but "kushi sambo"? what are we, fucking Victorians?

This racism isn't 50 years out of date, it's 200! Fuck, Israel, why are you being so stupid!

You're blowing it for all of us!

Part II: Towards a Black Jew

It didn't start out like that.

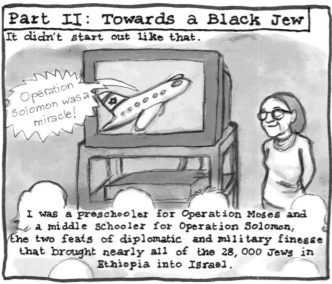

Operation Solomon was a miracle!

I was a preschooler for Operation Moses and a middle schooler for Operation Solomon, the two feats of diplomatic and military finesse that brought nearly all of the 28,000 Jews in Ethiopia into Israel.

I remember how amazing it all was.

Hearing about these black Jews, seeing the pictures of the arriving, joyous families—

—and in my school choir, singing a new song that tried *so hard* to rhyme.

We were dying in Africa, in the region of GON-dar, And our children were crying out, with disease and with HON-gar...

It was even more weird and wonderful for the kids in Israel.

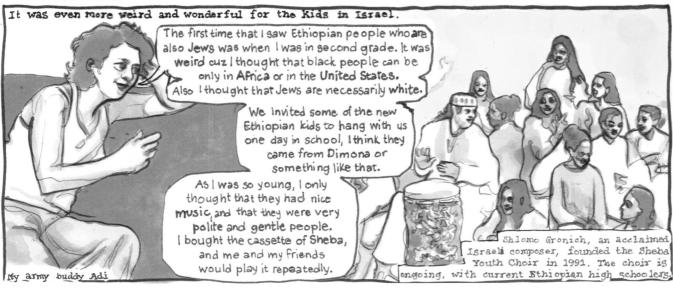

The first time that I saw Ethiopian people who are also Jews was when I was in second grade. It was weird cuz I thought that black people can be only in Africa or in the United States. Also I thought that Jews are necessarily white.

We invited some of the new Ethiopian kids to hang with us one day in school, I think they came from Dimona or something like that.

As I was so young, I only thought that they had nice music, and that they were very polite and gentle people. I bought the cassette of Sheba, and me and my friends would play it repeatedly.

My army buddy Adi

Shlomo Gronich, an acclaimed Israeli composer, founded the Sheba Youth Choir in 1991. The choir is ongoing, with current Ethiopian high schoolers.

Take it away, Dr. Ruth!

For hundreds of years, there existed in Ethiopia a people who called themselves the Beta Israel (the House of Israel), but were called by their neighbours Falasha (landless, wanderers). They practiced a peculiarly non-Talmudic form of Judaism, which included devotion to the Orit (the Ethiopic version of the Bible) but lacked most post-Biblical observances such as Chanukah, Purim, tallitoth (prayer shawls), kippoth (skull caps) teffilin (phylacteries), and Bar Mitzvah.

from her 1992 book Surviving Salvation with Steven Kaplan

The modern history of the Beta Israel can be said to begin in 1859 with the establishment in their midst of a Protestant mission under the auspices of the London Society for Promoting Christianity Among the Jews. The missionaries were the first group to treat the Beta Israel as 'Jews' in the universal sense.

The arrival in Ethiopia of Jacques Faitlovitch in 1904 marks a major turning point in the history of the Beta Israel. The common thread that ran through all aspects of his program on their behalf was the attempt to bring them closer to other Jewish communities. To this end, he sought to raise their standards of Education and created a Western-Educated elite capable of interacting on a more or less equal basis with their foreign Jewish counterparts. He also promoted an image of Ethiopian Jewry that was both familiar and attractive to European and American Jewish audiences.

In early 1973, the Israeli Ministry of Immigrant Absorption, having undertaken a comprehensive review of the situation, prepared a report calling for the cessation of all connections with the Beta Israel. Noting their ties to Ethiopia and the doubts raised concerning their status as Jews, it concluded that the Beta Israel were best left to fend for themselves in Ethiopia. Before the report was released, however, Ovadia Yosef, the Sephardi* chief rabbi, issued a religious ruling recognizing the Falasha as Jews. Citing rabbinic opinions from more than 400 years earlier, he stated that they were descendants of the lost tribe of Dan.

*(almost) a synonym of "Mizrahi": Mid-Eastern/North African Jews

Fleeing a famine in 1980, Jews from the relatively isolated regions of Tigre and Walqayit began to journey to the Sudan and settle in refugee camps.

By the middle of 1984, close to 10,000 Ethiopian Jews had crossed the border into Sudan. As the situation in the refugee camps deteriorated, the Israeli government decided to abandon its policy of gradual immigration in favour of a more ambitious policy. During a period of less than two months, more than 6,500 Ethiopian Jews were airlifted to Israel in what became known as 'Operation Moses.'

By the summer of 1990, amidst a rebellion that created violence throughout Ethiopia and was poised to topple the government, over 20,000 Ethiopian Jews had traveled to Addis Ababa in the hope of receiving exit visas. Many of the Jews in Addis Ababa had walked from Gondar, several hundred miles away.

In early 1991, Israeli negotiators led by Uri Lubrani sought to secure their rescue, while at the same time American officials including President George Bush's special envoy, former senator Rudy Boschwitz, attempted t put together a deal that would both secure the safety of the Beta Israel and limit bloodshed.

As rebel forces approached the capital, only one obstacle remained to be overcome before the Beta Israel could be released: money. Almost overnight, $35 million was raised and paid to the Ethiopian government. During 36 hours between May 24 and 25, over 14,000 Beta Israel were airlifted to Israel in 'Operation Solomon.'

More than a century after the Beta Israel were discovered as a Jewish community, I was privileged to play a central part in their redemption, and *Saving the Lost Tribe* is the story of Israel's and America's struggle to reunite the Falashas with the rest of Judaism and deliver them to the Holy Land.

Asher Naim, former Israeli ambassador to Ethiopia, from the introduction to his above-named memoir of Operation Solomon

This is where the story ends in the common telling.

Almost all of the books about Ethiopians in Israel available in English are twenty years old (ten years before I moved to Israel).

Some highlights of the last 20 years:

A gauntlet of (inconsistently applied) humiliations on arrival such as—

—wholesale changing of first names from Amharic to a small selection of biblical Hebrew ones—

EVE
SARAH
RIVKAH
RACHEL
LEAH
JUDITH
HANNAH

misting a planeful of refugees with bug spray (true!)

—compulsory mikvah* immersion—

*ritual "purifying" bath

—even recircumcision, although they were all recognized as Jews by the chief rabbinate—

After arrival: boarding schools that were culturally genocidal in the mould of schools for aboriginal children in the U.S. and Canada—

I was sent to a religious boarding school, where I worked very hard to become Israeli and also religious.

Whenever I knew something, the teachers were surprised because I am Ethiopian.

I wanted to go to university. But they expected us to become nothing more than cleaners.

Shula Mola, now Chairwoman of the Israel Association for Ethiopian Jews

—abysmal employment rates, including among the young and educated—

"Poverty is three times higher among Ethiopians than among other Jewish Israelis, and unemployment is twice as high." Newsweek, 2011

—the "blood riots" after Ethiopian-Israelis learned all the blood they donated was being thrown out as probably infected with AIDS—

—and overt, though illegal, housing discrimination.

...And in the year between researching and starting to draw this essay: the Israeli government admits to injecting hundreds of Ethiopian-Israeli woman with birth control, without their knowledge.

age-advanced artist's rendering

Even in the mostly fluffy coffee table book, *The Ethiopian Jews of Israel*, all the success stories fit a curiously narrow mould...

In 1984, Nigist Mengesha qualified for leaving Ethiopia with an offer to study at Ben Gurion University. In Israel, Nigist earned two advanced degrees in education.

In 2003, she was selected to become director general of the Ethiopian National Project, the first program of national scope addressing the needs of the Ethiopian community. This program was conceived by the **Jewish Agency for Israel and the United Jewish Communities.**

Tekele Mekonen is the director of Fidel ("alphabet" in Amharic), a nonprofit group focused on improving the elementary school environment for Ethiopian students.

Fidel trains and supervises mediators who bring elementary school teachers and Ethiopian parents together to improve primary school education. The majority of funds now come from the **American Jews—from the New York Federation, the Moriah Fund, and the New Israel Fund.**

In 2004, Mazi Melega was the elected chairperson of the Ethiopian National Students Organization, which represents the interests of the 2,300 Ethiopian Israeli university students.

Mazi was then a senior at the University of Haifa, planning to graduate with a degree in occupational therapy.

She was not optimistic about finding work in her field. As it turned out, Mazi was offered a job close to her heart: working in the **New York headquarters of the North American Conference on Ethiopian Jewry.**

Americans.

Why is it us founding and funding all these nonprofits?

Is it something in my **American heart** causing my seemingly misplaced guilt and indignant rage?

Why "blowing it for all of us"?

Is there some original **sin** I'm trying to expiate?

Or some original **vow** I'm trying to **fulfill?**

So. In the following pages, I will attempt to answer three questions:
1: Fuck, why are you being so stupid, 2: Why do I care, 3: What can be done.

Part III: The Black/Jewish Conspiracy

Like all Americans, American Jews have race on the brain.

We even have a short story about a long "special relationship" with African-Americans, repeated past the point of cliché:

Black spirituality was infused with Old Testament themes.

Jews and Blacks, from the 19th century onward, felt a kinship as two peoples freed from slavery.

A large fraction of the original NAACP was Jewish.

Schwerner and Goodman, the freedom summer martyrs.

Rabbi Heschel marched with Dr. King!

True, Jews and Blacks found solidarity and friendship through the similarity of their positions vis-a-vis American whites and the American definition of whiteness.

There's a great sense of community between Blacks and Jews in a city like Atlanta. We're all in the same boat. It's in our best interest to stick together.

Congressman John Lewis

But the differences between the roles they were cast into in White America never went away, and always caused discord when they popped up.

I suspect that if Mr. Chaney, who is a native Mississippian Negro, had been alone at the time of the disappearance, that this case, like so many others, would have gone completely unnoticed.

Rita Schwerner, widow of Mickey Schwerner

Jews protested country club exclusion when Blacks were protesting **lynching**.

Perhaps the two groups should understand that they may have very different notions about what it means to be oppressed.

Julius Lester

Middle-class Jewish housewives hired Black domestics on a daily basis, known as the "Bronx slave market."

In certain spots in the area, the Negro domestic workers gather each morning to be hired for daily work at rates that are sometimes as low as fifteen cents per hour. With the inevitable bundle under arm, they wait their turn to "sell" themselves to the housewives who often haggle and bid for the cheapest price.

L. D. Reddick

Jews were landlords and shopowners in African-American neighbourhoods.

It is a poor **excuse** for Jewish merchants who own the major downtown department stores, which set the policy in Baltimore, to say their patrons **force** them to employ discriminatory practices against Negroes.

Boycott and **picket** is the real solution to the problem. In this way we can call attention to the Jewish merchants who are guilty of Hitlerism here in Baltimore.

"Leading Negro Women of the Community," in a Black newspaper editorial, 1946

The NYC Afrocentric schools fight targeted Jewish administrators and teachers unions in its effort to reform Black students' curricula.

Then Israel's 1967 war came along and really ruined everything.

Jews gave up the **obligations** of remembered **victimhood** in the Biblical commandment "welcome the stranger, for you were strangers in **Egypt**" (the rallying cry of Jewish social **justice**)—

—and became **righteous** victims, soon righteous **avengers**.

"99 percent of all American Jews backed Israel's war aims. Jews who had not visited a synagogue in years crowded into them spontaneously and stood vigil at continuous services. As the threat of extinction became a miracle of triumph, American Jews let loose a torrent of joy and money that has not since abated." Taylor Branch

Black activists also started feeling their righteous aggrievitude, as a backlash against **King's** nonviolence and conciliation and as symbolic members of the third-world/nonwhite/subaltern global **community**

"A **SNCC Newsletter** article in fall **1967** stated that SNCC had 'placed itself squarely on the side of oppressed peoples and liberation movements... Perhaps we have taken the liberal Jewish community as far as it will go. If so, this is tragic, not for **us** but for the liberal Jewish community. Our message to conscious people everywhere is 'Don't get caught on the wrong side of the revolution.'" Clayborne Carson

In younger, more **militant** civil rights groups, Jews and other Whites were **cleansed** from leadership, and newsletters issued statements **condemning** Israel both in its recent **war** and for its very **foundation**.

"SNCC's veteran leaders came under strong attack from separatists. In place of an economic emphasis, they argued for the importance of racial identity; rather than to Marx, they looked to Franz Fanon or Malcolm X for ideological guidance. Rejecting the view that struggle was SNCC's reason for being, they insisted that ideological conversion was a necessary precondition for further struggles." Ibid

Afterward (amidst the trappings of **anti-assimilation** like more vocal Zionism and resurgence of Hebrew first **names**), Jews seemed to slide into being just another **White** community, with White residential patterns (affluent **suburbs ASAP**)—

"**Many** Chicago Blacks are doubtless correct in asserting that they have never seen a Jew, as Jews evacuated their neighbourhoods more than a generation **ago**." Taylor Branch, **1988**

—and White **concerns** (anti-busing, property values, tough-on-crime-itude).

"As Jews kept retreating to the edges of the city and beyond, the Negroes followed. This is a problem for the same reason that it is a problem for any White property owner or home-owner: fear of declining real estate values, fear of changes in the neighbourhood affecting the schools and homogeneity of the environment." Nathan Glazer, 1965

By the time I grew up, in an Orthodox enclave in the nicest suburb of Columbus, Ohio, my family was **unquestionably** White People.

"Jews are more likely than **other** Whites to be **upset** if Blacks move into their neighbourhood.

20% of Jews said they did not want their **children** to attend school with **Blacks**, compared with only 14% of other Whites."
—LC Pogrebin, 1991

I didn't **mix** at all with Blacks besides Gene, the kindly, grizzled janitor at my school—

—Mr. Ed, who taught all my art classes at the local community centre in middle and high school—

Gene undoubtedly had a last name, and Mr. Ed was **Ed Colston**, a celebrated and successful local artist, but we **kids** always called them by their first names as per White-American convention.

—and my cousins who lived in Washington, DC.

My Jewish private school was 99% White, without really even Sephardim to speak of.

Yet kinship with **nonwhites** and oppressed groups was part of our origin story. The denomination-bridging **Rabbi Heschel** is in the DNA of all American Jews.

We heard **vaguely** that it fell **apart**.

Still, the historical education which is **central** in US Jewish schools meant that we never stopped being reminded how **nonwhite** we were really, and how those in **power** could turn on us any minute.

Explicitly **allying** ourselves with **Whites** against Blacks and immigrants seemed—

(to most of us, I thought)

—like a naïve, stupid **trap.**

This is the ambivalent atmosphere in which "saving the black Jews" became the favourite cause: American Jews' last and best chance to make good with all of black-kind, to have Blacks who would be our brothers really, who would be ours as we would be theirs.

Operation Solomon was a miracle!

All we had to do was chip in our money and influence, and we'd gotten really good at that.

General Brent Snowcroft, US national security adviser, agreed to send Mengistu a letter from President Bush to ask for the release of the Falashas as a humanitarian gesture, Simcha Dinitz, chairman of the Jewish Agency, put forward Senator Rudy Boschwitz as the president's emissary to personally deliver the letter. American diplomatic muscle plus American Jewish money would be enormously persuasive.

Dinitz had raised thirty-five million dollars in New York a month earlier, explaining that the money was needed to save the Jews of Ethiopia. He admitted it was a ransom, but Dinitz said we had been paying ransom to redeem Jewish lives throughout our history. The executive vice president of the UJF called various philanthropic groups and they raised the amount in days.

The government agreed to let the Falashas go under three conditions 1: that the operation be clandestine 2: that Ethiopia Airlines carry out the flights. 3: that Ethiopia be given a "generous financial contribution."

The American Jewish communities are like Moses for us. They helped us with their power and money to bring us out of Ethiopia and to reach our Promised Land.

Asher Naim, on the coordination of the massive Operation Solomon airlift

Kess Avihu Azariah, Ethiopian-Israeli religious leader

We would have gotten away with it, too, if it hadn't been for those meddling Israelis!

All they needed to do was integrate the Ethiopians as equals, and create the totally colourblind Jewish country we always trumpet.

How hard could that be?

Part IV: Against Jewish Blacks

What about the Israelis then? Is being Israeli semiotically (that is, in a system that assigns generally-agreed-upon symbolic meaning) Black, or White?

Are they playing the role of oppressors or oppressed, and how does this dictate how they (the giant meta-they) act?

postmodernist hat

19th-and early-20th-century European-Jewish thinkers drew the same parallels between themselves and African-Americans that American Jews did.

ABUSE OF POWER COMES AS NO SURPRISE

But neither Marxist nor modernist philosophical/theological anti-racism seemed to survive the journey to Palestine... as some of the thinkers who had stayed in Europe observed.

Human beings, merely because they were black, were stolen like cattle, captured and sold... I wish also to assist in the redemption of the Africans.

Labor in the white skin can never free itself as long as labor in the black skin is branded.

My slavery in Egypt constitutes my very humanity, a fact that allies me to the workers, the wretched, and the persecuted people of the world.

Theodore Herzl

Karl Marx

Emmanuel Levinas

Perhaps we should derive from the Diaspora something more than the qualities of farmers and soldiers.

Levinas again, 1960

This -um- lack of effort toward anti-racism is seen in depictions of (and arguably, dealings with) Palestinian Arabs, which continue to reverberate through the region.

"Now my attitude is this. I do not hate them and I do not love them; I do not wish to see their faces. In my humble opinion, we must build a large ghetto of half a million Jews in Palestine." Author S.Y. Agnon after the 1929 clashes.

But there is an equally fateful, less-discussed original sin of the early Zionist state: the Mizrahi Aliyah (mass immigration of Jews from Arab/Muslim countries) of the '40s and '50s.

The **contrast** between **Ashkenazi** (European/Western) immigrant experiences, like those of the Holocaust refugees, and the experiences of **Mizrahi** populations a few years later, couldn't be more **striking**—

—from the stereotypical **codename** of the airlift of Yemeni Jews in 1949, "Operation **Magic Carpet**," to **settlement** policy where kibbutzim got **arable** land and government **grants**—

—and Mizrahim got "**peripheral** communities" in the deserts where many of them **remain** to this day.

As the absorption facilities became **exhausted** the authorities constructed "**development towns**" in frontier regions. Although Israeli propaganda **lauded** the Ashkenazi kibbutzim for their courage, Sephardi border settlements lacked the strong infrastructure of **military protection** provided to Ashkenazim, leading to Sephardi **loss of life**.

Ella Shohat, Iraqi-Israeli-American postcolonialist theorist

We do not want Israelis to become Arabs. We are duty-bound to fight the spirit of the Levant, which corrupts individuals and societies, and preserve the authentic Jewish values as they crystallized in the diaspora.

The object should be to infuse [the Sephardim] with an Occidental spirit, rather than allow them to drag us into an unnatural Orientalism.

David Ben-Gurion

Abba Eban

The binary that set in was as banal as it was evil. Religious Mizrahim, who immigrated in close-knit communities (not solitary refugees like the Holocaust survivors, or idealistic runaways like the kibbutznikim), came to represent the weak, superstitious ancestors the "new Jews" "evolved" from. Ashkenazic thought despised about the Mizrahim everything it despised about its own parents. Simultaneously, the Mizrahim's "Middle Easternness" represented everything that frightened and confused Ashkenazim about their adopted land.

So **they** became semiotically **white** and the **Mizrahim** became semiotically **black**.
(Both groups are genetically diverse, and can't always be distinguished visually.)

The dichotomy is an original sin in the sense that it has tainted aspects of Israeli society ever since, notably that left-wing parties are so linked with the old kibbutz movement that they are ipso facto ethnic parties.

Speaking to a Labour rally during the 1999 elections, Barak supporter actress Tiki Dayan referred to working-class Likud voters as asafsuf, Hebrew for "riff-raff."

Likud candidate Netanyahu seized on the slur, shouting it in a campaign appearance in Beersheba. "I am a proud asafsuf!" the prime minister told the crowd.

At worst, left-party leaders don't hide their contempt for Mizrahim, while at best, they downplay their forebears' role in Mizrahi marginalization.

The dominant socialist-humanist discourse in Israel hides wealth and poverty behind a facade of egalitarianism.

The May Day celebrations and their speeches in the name of the "working class" mask the fact that the labour network really represents only the interests of the Ashkenazi elite.

Shohat again

Two generations after the great immigrations, the poorest Israeli Jews were Mizrahim, while the richest were Ashkenazi (ditto for least/most educated, most/least likely to be in jail, etc.).

Ashkenazim have double the representation in white-collar occupations. Their attendance rate is **five times** as high in universities.

Sephardim, despite their majority status [in 1988], are **under-represented** in the government, in the Knesset, in the higher echelons of the military, in the media, and in academia. They are over-represented in the marginal, stigmatized regions of professional and social life.

Still, Mizrahim did achieve all levels of society, if not in an equal way to Ashkenazim. Mizrahi cultures make the cuisine, ritual art, and music designated "authentically Israeli."

Ashkenazim and Mizrahim are enthusiastically intergamous, and standard Israeli Hebrew splits the difference between Yiddish- and Arabic-inflected pronunciation.

My apartment at the military prep program my first year in Israel: two Ashkenazim, two half-Mizrahim.

When **Ethiopian** Jews were imported in the 80s, there needed to be a **box** they could fit into, in this metanarrative—

(postmodern-speak for a story a culture tells itself **about** itself, that all other stories **conform** to)

—this uneasy **détente** between dark, authentic Mizrahim and white, culturally impoverished **Ashkenazim**.

ABUSE OF POWER COMES NO SURPRISE

Did Mizrahim feel they had a symbolic **kinship** with Ethiopians, as "nonwhite" Jews? **Maybe.** North-African-born Jews were **essential** to the Beta Israel immigration.

Ovadia Yosef (then Sephardi chief rabbi, later Mizrahi pride advocate and "spiritual leader" of the Orthodox party SHAS) **first** ruled Beta Israel were **Jews** according to Jewish law.

There's **Ovadia Hezi**, Eritrean-born Yemeni Jew and iconic IDF Sergeant major. On a trip **back** to Eritrea in 1966, he reconnected with the Beta Israel community and soon founded many of the first **organizations** for their immigration and absorption. In 1971, he **brought** the case to Rabbi Yosef that the Beta Israel **had** to be **recognized** as Jews.

And **Asher Naim**, the Tunisian-born Israeli diplomat who **coordinated** the daring mass exodus of **Operation Solomon.**

Names for refugee airlifts had gotten less offensively **stereotypical** since the days of Operation **Magic Carpet**... luckily, or we might have had Operation the **GODS must be crazy**

At last, a comedy everyone can laugh with!

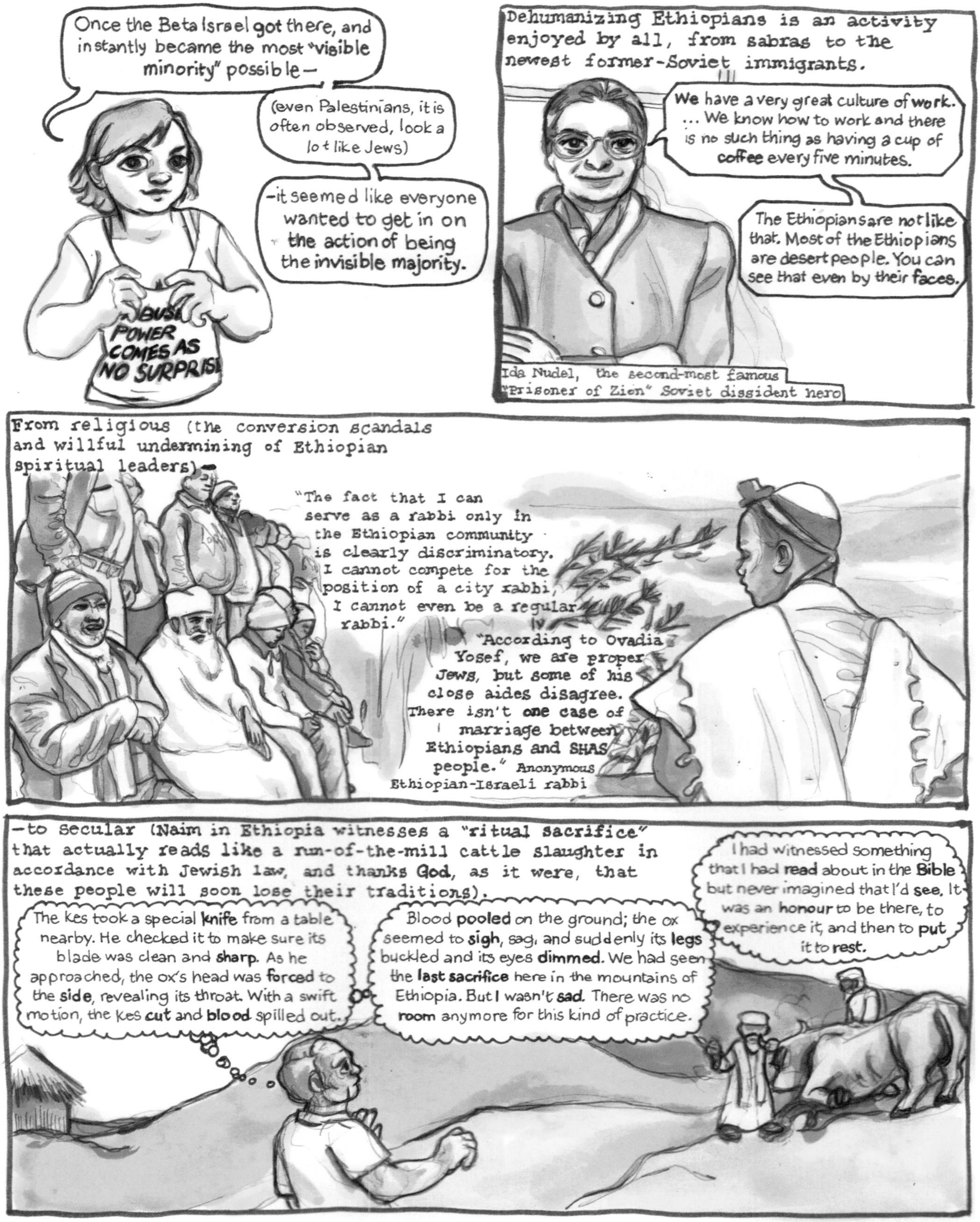
Once the Beta Israel got there, and instantly became the most "visible minority" possible—
(even Palestinians, it is often observed, look a lot like Jews)
—it seemed like everyone wanted to get in on the action of being the invisible majority.
BUSI
POWER
COMES AS
NO SURPRIS
Dehumanizing Ethiopians is an activity enjoyed by all, from sabras to the newest former-Soviet immigrants.
We have a very great culture of work. ... We know how to work and there is no such thing as having a cup of coffee every five minutes.
The Ethiopians are not like that. Most of the Ethiopians are desert people. You can see that even by their faces.
Ida Nudel, the second-most famous "Prisoner of Zion" Soviet dissident hero
From religious (the conversion scandals and willful undermining of Ethiopian spiritual leaders)—
"The fact that I can serve as a rabbi only in the Ethiopian community is clearly discriminatory. I cannot compete for the position of a city rabbi, I cannot even be a regular rabbi."
"According to Ovadia Yosef, we are proper Jews, but some of his close aides disagree. There isn't one case of marriage between Ethiopians and SHAS people." Anonymous Ethiopian-Israeli rabbi
—to secular (Naim in Ethiopia witnesses a "ritual sacrifice" that actually reads like a run-of-the-mill cattle slaughter in accordance with Jewish law, and thanks God, as it were, that these people will soon lose their traditions).
The kes took a special knife from a table nearby. He checked it to make sure its blade was clean and sharp. As he approached, the ox's head was forced to the side, revealing its throat. With a swift motion, the kes cut and blood spilled out.
Blood pooled on the ground; the ox seemed to sigh, sag, and suddenly its legs buckled and its eyes dimmed. We had seen the last sacrifice here in the mountains of Ethiopia. But I wasn't sad. There was no room anymore for this kind of practice.
I had witnessed something that I had read about in the Bible but never imagined that I'd see. It was an honour to be there, to experience it, and then to put it to rest.

Degradation ripples from the most powerful—

(government policies like pointlessly spraying planefuls of immigrants with insecticide, and later revelations that all Ethiopian blood donations were being thrown out on "suspicion of AIDS")

—to the least.

The kids I saw spit on the Ethiopian soldier-teacher were all Mizrahim living well below the poverty line.

The most recent scandal of housing discrimination against Ethiopians came from Kiryat Malachi, one of those historically poor and historically Mizrahi development towns.

Racism

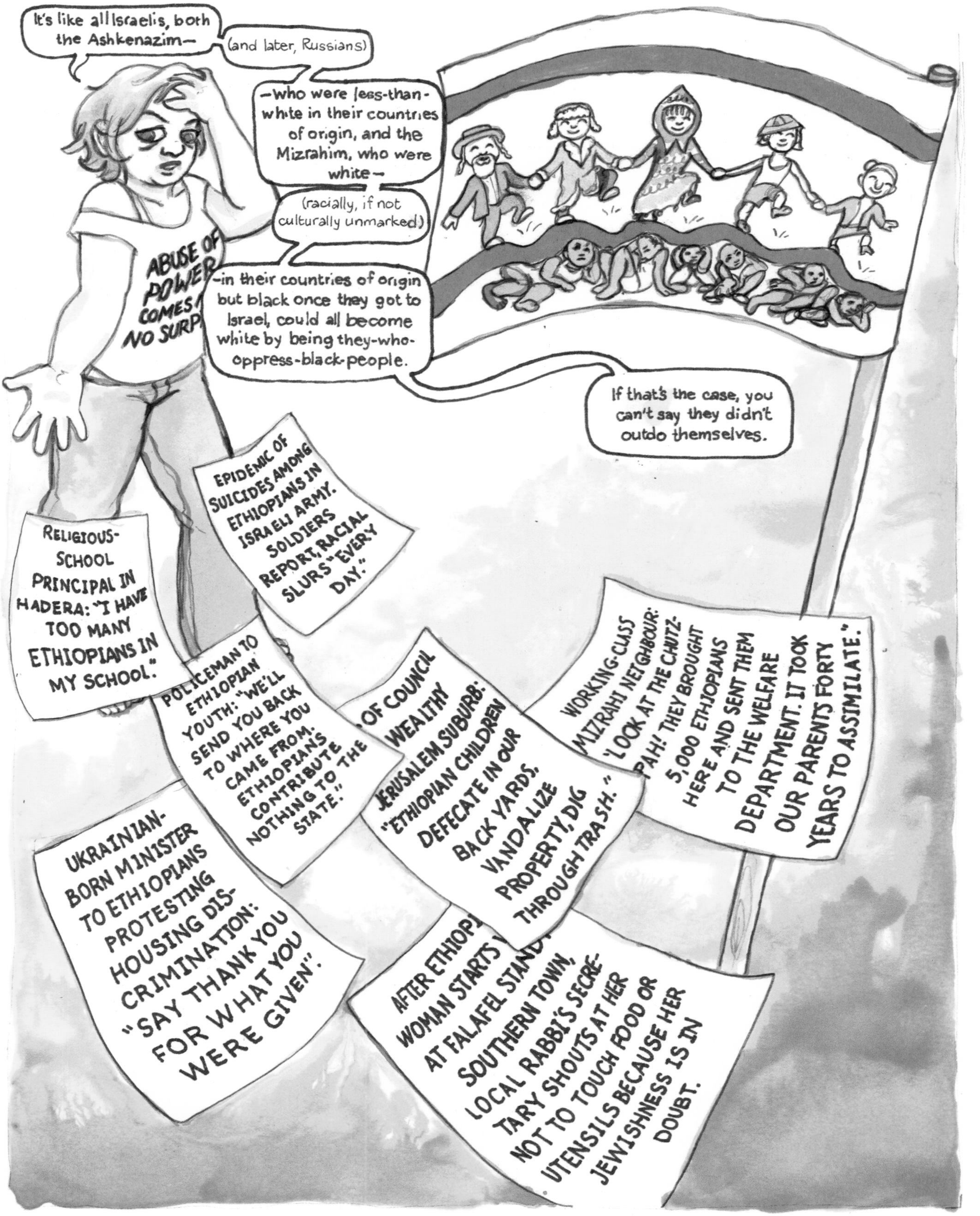
It's like all Israelis, both the Ashkenazim—
(and later, Russians)
—who were less-than-white in their countries of origin, and the Mizrahim, who were white—
(racially, if not culturally unmarked)
—in their countries of origin but black once they got to Israel, could all become white by being they-who-oppress-black-people.
If that's the case, you can't say they didn't outdo themselves.
ABUSE OF POWER COMES A NO SURP
EPIDEMIC OF SUICIDES AMONG ETHIOPIANS IN ISRAELI ARMY. SOLDIERS REPORT RACIAL SLURS "EVERY DAY."
RELIGIOUS-SCHOOL PRINCIPAL IN HADERA: "I HAVE TOO MANY ETHIOPIANS IN MY SCHOOL."
POLICEMAN TO ETHIOPIAN YOUTH: "WE'LL SEND YOU BACK TO WHERE YOU CAME FROM. ETHIOPIANS CONTRIBUTE NOTHING TO THE STATE."
OF COUNCIL WEALTHY JERUSALEM SUBURB: "ETHIOPIAN CHILDREN DEFECATE IN OUR BACK YARDS, VANDALIZE PROPERTY, DIG THROUGH TRASH."
WORKING-CLASS MIZRAHI NEIGHBOUR: 'LOOK AT THE CHUTZ-PAH! THEY BROUGHT 5,000 ETHIOPIANS HERE AND SENT THEM TO THE WELFARE DEPARTMENT. IT TOOK OUR PARENTS FORTY YEARS TO ASSIMILATE.'
UKRAINIAN-BORN MINISTER TO ETHIOPIANS PROTESTING HOUSING DIS-CRIMINATION: "SAY THANK YOU FOR WHAT YOU WERE GIVEN".
AFTER ETHIOPI WOMAN STARTS AT FALAFEL STAND SOUTHERN TOWN, LOCAL RABBI'S SECRE-TARY SHOUTS AT HER NOT TO TOUCH FOOD OR UTENSILS BECAUSE HER JEWISHNESS IS IN DOUBT.

Part V: When Blacks Were Jews

POSTMODERN CUL[...]

METANARRATIVE- a narr[...]
mythology of a cultur[...]
culture's ideas

SEMIOTICS- the study of culturally-agr[...]
symbols

SIMULACRUM- a copy/reenactment wit[...]
imaginary) original

HEGEMONY- a ruling class whi[...]
absolute worldview

SUBALTERN- an oppressed pers[...]
voice or agency

Human groups create overarching **mythologies** to assign meaning to our **existence** and the existence of people who are **not us**.

But as complicated as these stories are—

Ham was cursed by God for looking at Noah's nakedness and his descendants became **dark-skinned**;

His son Canaan was cursed by God, and his descendants became **slaves**.

Which means God asked personally for every Black person to be enslaved!

—they seem to constantly boil down to the simplest binary oppositions.

People who are not us become the **Other**, with a limited range of possible relationships to the Us. This is known as—

Flexible positional superiority

—in Edward Said's pioneering work, *Orientalism*. Explained by Ella Shohat as—

—putting the Westerner in a series of possible relations with the Oriental, but without the Westerner ever losing the relative upper hand.

Are Orientalisms **inevitable**? The minute a group gets a bit of power, does it automatically develop a self-conception that forces another group to be its despised opposite, the black to its white, the primitive to its advanced?

Can humans conceive of unfamiliar others as anything but "objects of contrast," and ultimately simulacra, our relations with each other an imitation of something that was never real to begin with?

Of course, race itself, and ethnic character, are not real in the biological sense.
Orientalism made it possible to talk about how truisms about groups are constructed.

By studying the history and metamorphoses of these truisms, postcolonial studies shows their falsity, whose interests the mythology serves, and how.

Postmodernism then developed the tools to discuss the mythologies (metanarratives) and systems of symbolism (semiotics) which have no objective truth, but create facts on the ground.

Colonialism is not satisfied merely with holding a people in its grip and emptying the native's brain of all form and content.

By a kind of perverted logic, it turns to the past of the oppressed people, and distorts, disfigures, and destroys it.

Frantz Fanon

Said showed how "the **East**" was created as an **idea**, as the binary **opposite** and dark **shadow** of "the West" in the West's own **imagination**—

—which translated into **policies** and regimes that ended up **dictating** a great deal of the lives of the **real** people **living** in the Middle East and Asia.

Applying *Orientalism*-style **analysis** to any "clash of civilizations," one can see the **same** script followed to tragically **ridiculous** conclusions.

In medieval Europe, **Jews** were the polar opposite of Christians, the **darkness** to their light, the evil to their good.

Why are most Gentiles fair-skinned and handsome while most Jews are dark and ugly? This is similar to fruit; when it begins to grow it is white, but when it ripens it becomes black.

dark mirror of Christendom

Medieval Jewish apologia

As sub-Saharan **Africans** and Native Americans were discovered by European consciousness, **their** strangeness was analogized to **Judaism**.

Amerigo Vespucci

They [Native Americans] can be called neither Moors nor Jews, but worse than Gentiles.

In other words, when Jews were **black** in Europe, Blacks were **Jews**.

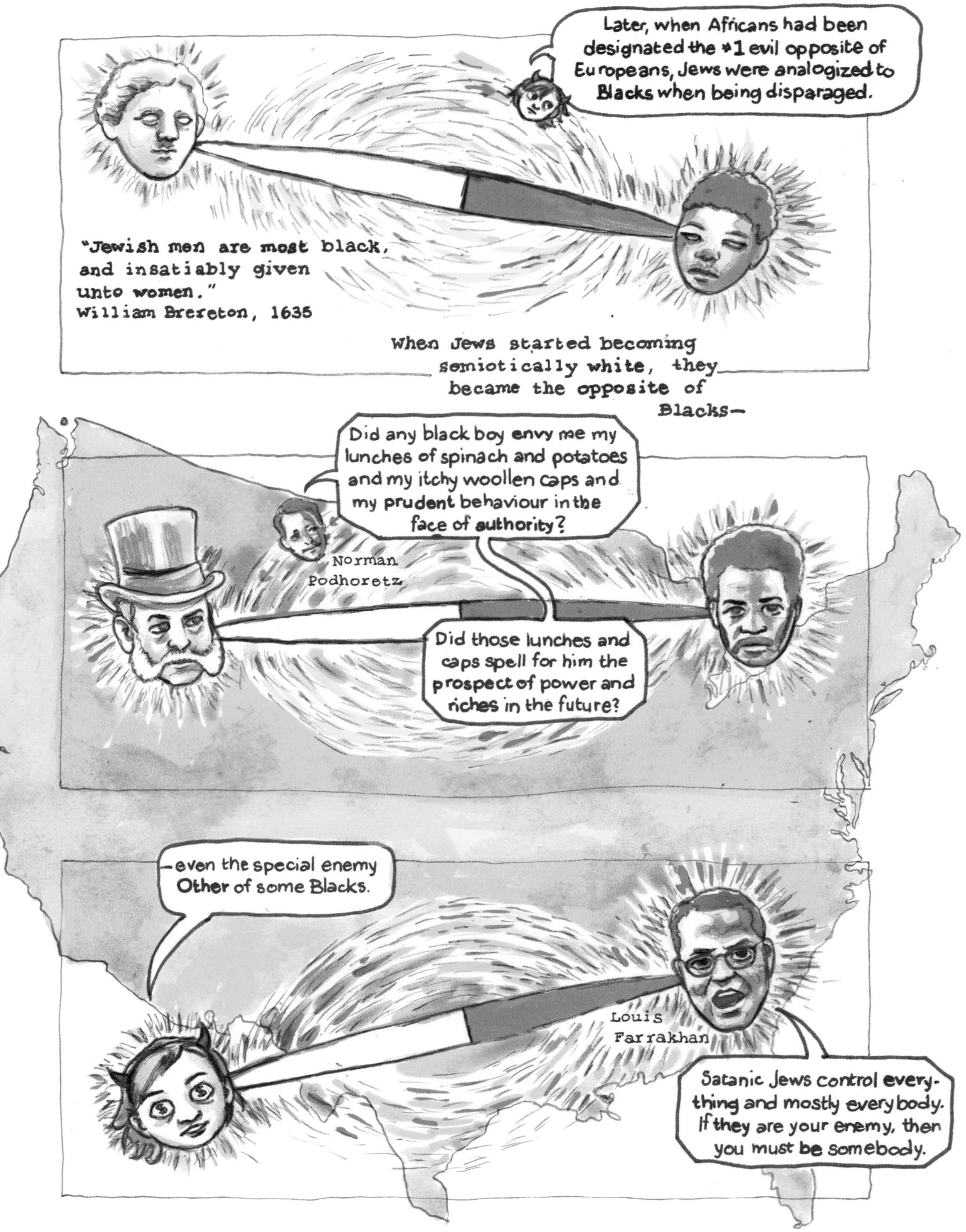
Later, when Africans had been designated the #1 evil opposite of Europeans, Jews were analogized to Blacks when being disparaged.
"Jewish men are most black, and insatiably given unto women."
William Brereton, 1635
When Jews started becoming semiotically white, they became the opposite of Blacks—
Did any black boy envy me my lunches of spinach and potatoes and my itchy woollen caps and my prudent behaviour in the face of authority?
Norman Podhoretz
Did those lunches and caps spell for him the prospect of power and riches in the future?
—even the special enemy Other of some Blacks.
Louis Farrakhan
Satanic Jews control everything and mostly everybody. If they are your enemy, then you must be somebody.

Back in Ohio, we reenacted our prescribed roles.

That's ridiculous! Both you and I know he never stole anything! We have to **do** something about this!!

As in the age-old plot, Gene the kindly school janitor was framed for an insignificant theft and fired.

All my family did was hire him to mow our lawn.

Which lasted for maybe a couple of summers.

Meanwhile, at school...

...and suddenly there were like ten *schvartzes* standing around and probably with like guns—

I know! But you can't say 'schvartze' in New York. They know what it means!

It's true! My uncle told me—

We had become white and they had become black, and we were all simulacra to each other.

Once Jewish philanthropy had been almost completely freed from helping our former black brothers, we dumped barrelsful of money on our new, better black brothers...

1950s survey found that "one in five Jews thought being a good Jew meant to support Israel. Twice as many believed it essential to support the Negroes' struggle in America."

By 1989, 73% of American Jews agreed that "caring about Israel is a very important part of being a Jew."

$600 million for Ethiopian Jews since 1991, by common estimate.

For all the good it ultimately did.

After 20 years, with Ethiopian-Israeli poverty three times as high as the national average, unemployment twice as high, and only 15% of Ethiopian-Israeli university graduates working in the field they trained in (!), Susan Pollack, founder of Friends of Ethiopian Jews, confessed, "There's been this attitude that we just need to give money to the Israelis and they'll know what to do. Considering the effort and money expended over the years, we should be seeing much better results."

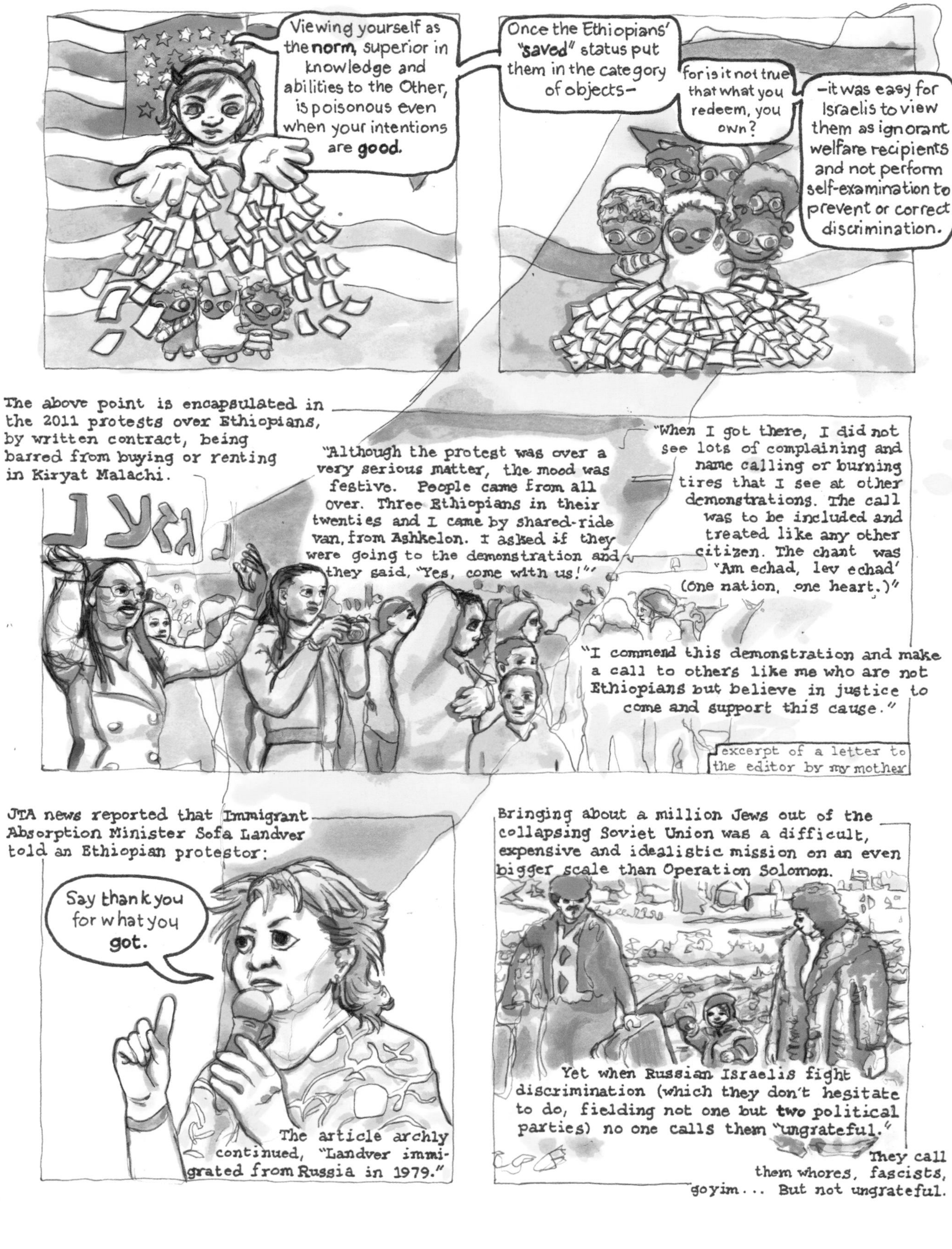
Viewing yourself as the norm, superior in knowledge and abilities to the Other, is poisonous even when your intentions are good.
Once the Ethiopians' "saved" status put them in the category of objects—
for is it not true that what you redeem, you own?
—it was easy for Israelis to view them as ignorant welfare recipients and not perform self-examination to prevent or correct discrimination.
The above point is encapsulated in the 2011 protests over Ethiopians, by written contract, being barred from buying or renting in Kiryat Malachi.
"Although the protest was over a very serious matter, the mood was festive. People came from all over. Three Ethiopians in their twenties and I came by shared-ride van, from Ashkelon. I asked if they were going to the demonstration and they said, "Yes, come with us!""
"When I got there, I did not see lots of complaining and name calling or burning tires that I see at other demonstrations. The call was to be included and treated like any other citizen. The chant was "Am echad, lev echad' (One nation, one heart.)"
"I commend this demonstration and make a call to others like me who are not Ethiopians but believe in justice to come and support this cause."
excerpt of a letter to the editor by my mother
JTA news reported that Immigrant Absorption Minister Sofa Landver told an Ethiopian protestor:
Say thank you for what you got.
The article archly continued, "Landver immigrated from Russia in 1979."
Bringing about a million Jews out of the collapsing Soviet Union was a difficult, expensive and idealistic mission on an even bigger scale than Operation Solomon.
Yet when Russian Israelis fight discrimination (which they don't hesitate to do, fielding not one but two political parties) no one calls them "ungrateful."
They call them whores, fascists, goyim... But not ungrateful.

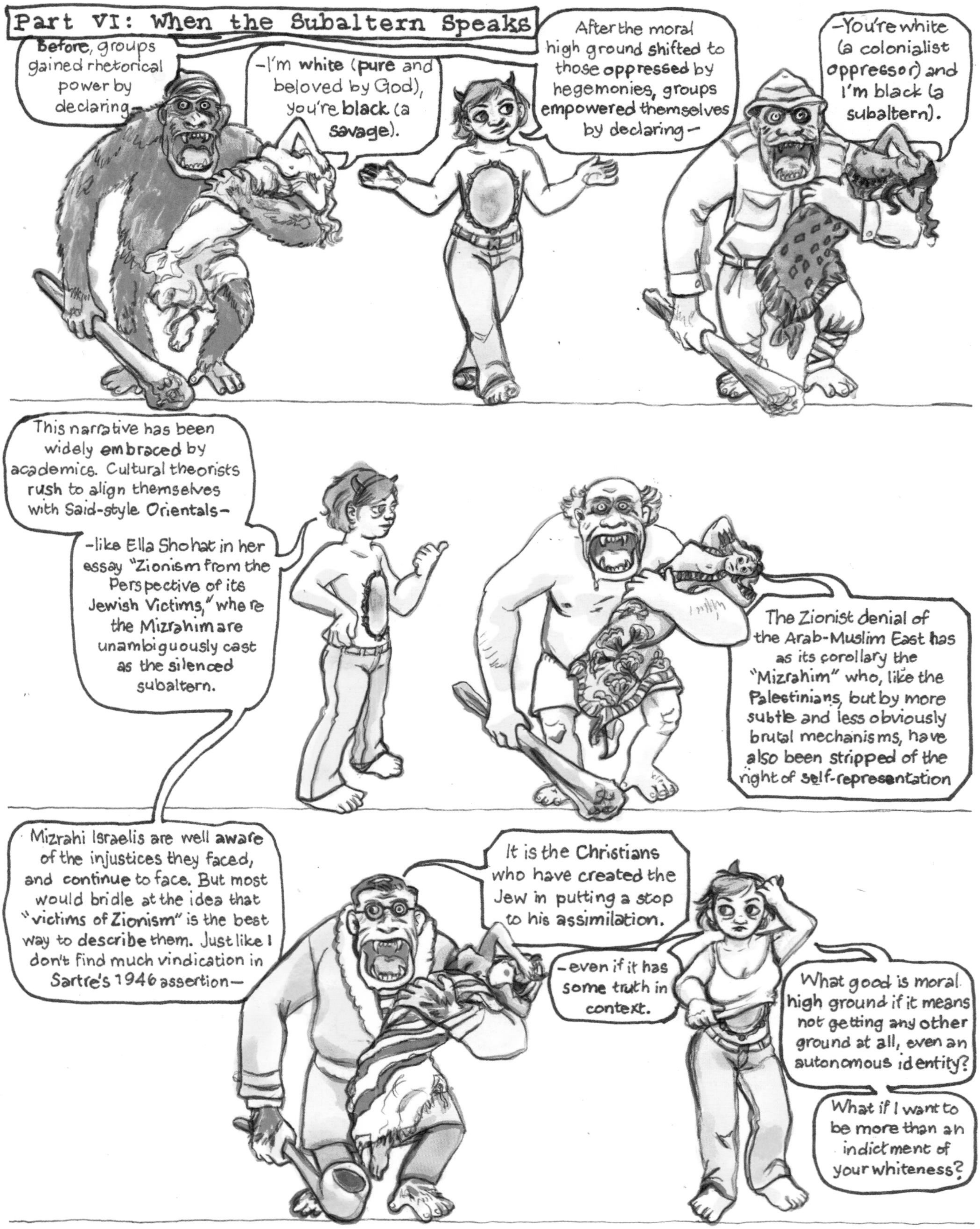
Part VI: When the Subaltern Speaks
Before, groups gained rhetorical power by declaring—
—I'm white (pure and beloved by God), you're black (a savage).
After the moral high ground shifted to those oppressed by hegemonies, groups empowered themselves by declaring—
—You're white (a colonialist oppressor) and I'm black (a subaltern).
This narrative has been widely embraced by academics. Cultural theorists rush to align themselves with Said-style Orientals—
—like Ella Shohat in her essay "Zionism from the Perspective of its Jewish Victims," where the Mizrahim are unambiguously cast as the silenced subaltern.
The Zionist denial of the Arab-Muslim East has as its corollary the "Mizrahim" who, like the Palestinians, but by more subtle and less obviously brutal mechanisms, have also been stripped of the right of self-representation
Mizrahi Israelis are well aware of the injustices they faced, and continue to face. But most would bridle at the idea that "victims of Zionism" is the best way to describe them. Just like I don't find much vindication in Sartre's 1946 assertion—
It is the Christians who have created the Jew in putting a stop to his assimilation.
—even if it has some truth in context.
What good is moral high ground if it means not getting any other ground at all, even an autonomous identity?
What if I want to be more than an indictment of your whiteness?

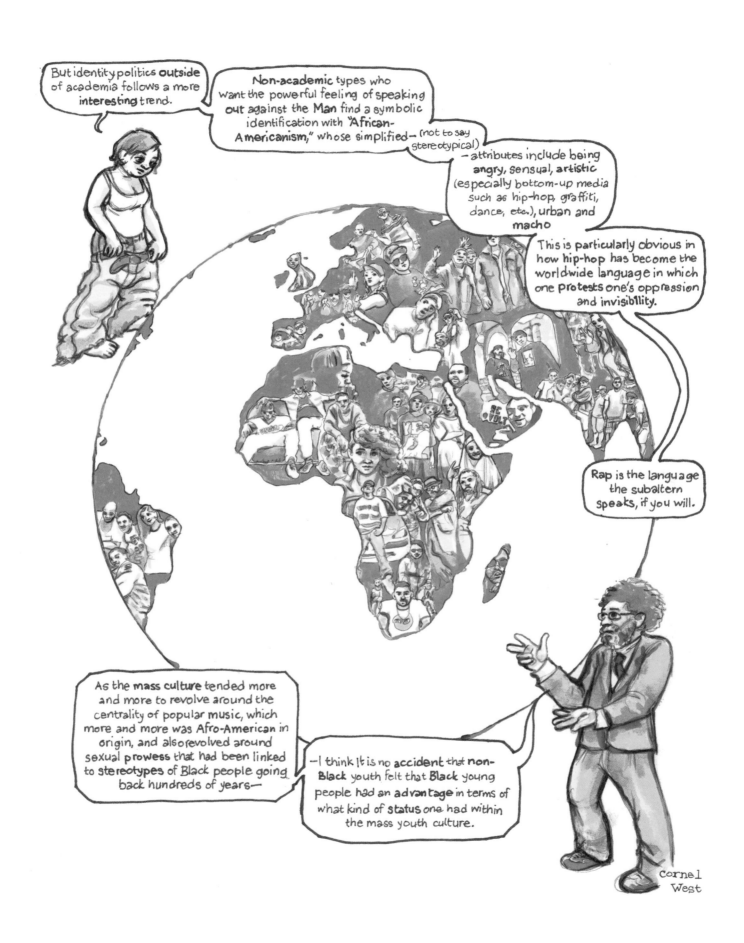

But identity politics **outside** of academia follows a more **interesting** trend.

Non-academic types who want the powerful feeling of speaking out against the Man find a symbolic identification with "African-Americanism," whose simplified— (not to say stereotypical)

—attributes include being **angry, sensual, artistic** (especially bottom-up media such as hip-hop, graffiti, dance, etc.), urban and macho

This is particularly obvious in how hip-hop has become the worldwide language in which one **protests** one's oppression and invisibility.

Rap is the language the subaltern speaks, if you will.

As the **mass culture** tended more and more to revolve around the centrality of popular music, which more and more was Afro-American in origin, and also revolved around sexual **prowess** that had been linked to **stereotypes** of Black people going back hundreds of years—

—I think it is no accident that **non-Black** youth felt that Black young people had an **advantage** in terms of what kind of **status** one had within the mass youth culture.

Cornel West

118

I remember African-Americanism seeming very inspirational to Ethiopian-Israeli kids when I lived there.

Many Israeli thinkers recoiled at the "scary" image these formerly "gentle people" chose to project.

Why should they be Black? Why don't they want to be Jewish?

One sees boys in body-hugging white shirts and oversized trousers.

The girls, wearing low-cut white pants revealing their midriffs and bedecked with jewellery, hang around with the boys and smoke.

Uri Ben-Eliezer

This colour consciousness is manifest among the youth who adopt Afro-American models in their music, hairstyle, and clothing.
There is a threat of a black counter-culture at the margins of Israeli society.

Lisa Anteby-Yemini

They wore leather pants, high heels and short-sleeved black shirts. Their hair was tinted blonde.

They had transformed from the Ethiopian girls I had met in Addis. They seemed to have lost their innocence.

Asher Naim

But if the donning of African-Americanism is not about race, but about resisting the Man, that explains the other Jewish groups who try it on—

—from Russian Israelis—

—to Ashkenazi youth—

—to urban American Jews.

Vulkan's surprise hit "Ha-Aliyah" (immigration) about prejudice in Israel

who can grow Afros and dreadlocks more readily than your average white person

The Beastie Boys, Lyor Cohen, and Rick Rubin in on the ground floor of the hip-hop boom

Part VII: Can the Alter-Altern Speak?

African-Americanism, then, is not precisely a subaltern identity. It's about being a minority, and maybe having less, but also an indomitable strength **not** based in victimhood. Other hegemony-resisting identities exist in the world, though.

Dozens of groups in all corners of Africa, from Senegal to Madagascar, align themselves with a "**Jewish essence**" kind of like the above-described "**American Black essence**," distinguishing themselves from their respective **majority** cultures.

In 2002, about 400 members of the **Abayudaya** community in Uganda were **converted** to Judaism by US and Israeli conservative **rabbis**.

Prof. Edith Bruder

The originator of the Abayudaya was Samei Lwakilenzi Kakungulu, a brilliant military chief who converted to **Protestantism** in the 1880s, and then adapted his **own** version of Old-Testament-based religion in 1919, which came to resemble **rabbinic Judaism** more and more closely.

A missionary in the 1920s observed, "Kakungulu is a chief of considerable means and **influence** so that he is able to build schools... The teachers wear turbans like the **Jews** of old times. They observe Saturday as a day of **rest** and keep it much more strictly than the **Christians** do their **Sunday**."

"The Luba administrative, social, and commercial elite have spread over the Congo to form an ethnic **Diaspora** viewed with suspicion. As early as the 1960s, the Baluba regarded themselves as the '**Jews of the Congo**'" United States Institute of Peace.

"Tens of thousands of Blacks in South Africa, Zimbabwe and Mozambique are claiming **descent** from lost **biblical tribes**. The **Lemba** people say they originated around AD 600 from a Jewish tribe in **Yemen**." Pretoria Times, 1986

Prof. Jean Bwejeri

The **Tutsi** in Rwanda may be the most semiotically **fascinating** of these groups.

Tutsi-Hutu animosity traces back to European colonizers declaring the Tutsi minority more "**advanced**"— (including theories that they descended from wandering Jews)

—and elevating them to an **overclass**.

During the genocide, the Tutsis **themselves** called back to the connection with **Judaism**.

Hugh Stayt, 1930s ethnographer, testified that the Lemba had "marked **Semitic** characteristics," absorbed the languages of where they settled, but maintained "the **purity** of their race." Stayt asserted the "life of these peculiar people is strangely reminiscent of the wandering Jews of medieval times," meaning the Lemba's practice of trading rather than farming. They were also "**feared** for their superior intelligence."

For the last 40 years, the Batutsi have been exterminated and are **being** exterminated because of their **Hebraic** identity and Solomonic **legacy**.

The Judaism emulated here is not the brash, **macho** Judaism that is stereotypical of contemporary Israelis, which Zionist ideologues insist should replace "weak, **ghetto**" identities...

Very few "African Israelites" seek Israeli citizenship.

It is specifically a **diaspora** Judaism, where you are not the **majority** in your God-given **homeland**, but a minority, who has to figure out how to live **safely** without disappearing.

Thus Jewish-ism as a group identity entails being persecuted—

—(though sometimes wealthy) —

—because you are meek, refined, brainy, and—dare you say—a cut a bove the people around you.

A joke:

If we Jews are **5%** better than the rest of the world, we can be "a light unto the nations." If we are **25%** better than the rest of the world, we can bring the Messiah. If we're **50%** better than the rest of the world, we'll all be dead.

"Rabbi Greenberg," quoted by Joseph Telushkin

The European missionaries who first "studied" Beta Israel in the 19th century reported that they were disdained by their neighbours for being medical practitioners and craftspeople instead of farmers.

A later ethnologist related that "Ethiopians say they can recognize a Falasha by the heavy mineral odour of water that clings to him as a result of his incessant ritual ablutions."

It's hard to imagine stigmas more gratifying to a Victorian audience!

This identity does have a whiff of civilized-against-primitive, one facet of Orientalism.

Does that mean people who take on Jewish-ism are calling themselves white among the black? I don't think so.

Many early-20th century Jewish intellectuals depicted the neighbouring Ukrainian peasants in an idealizing-infantilizing "noble savage" vein.

Ukrainian peasants! Who were super-white, and also freely committing **pogroms** against Jews.

Parse *that* with a gorilla.

WEB DuBois and the NAACP publicly embraced Jewish figures for their fundraising abilities and legal expertise, and often looked to American Jews, not American Whites or African/Caribbean populations, for emulation.

Jews were their example of people who moved in White society, taking education and success in the professions, while maintaining pride in their unique culture, and not being quiet (in the media or the legal realm) about discrimination.

The Jew has been made international by persecution and forced dispersion. And so, potentially, have we.

Alain Locke

The African Hebrew Israelites of Chicago and Dimona, Israel, are the most obvious example of African Americans adopting elements of a Jewish identity to escape the pain of a subalterity, without aligning with the oppressor identity (Whiteness).

But on the micro level, individual Americans have come to Judaism as a way, partly, of escaping the bind of being White or Black.

In addition to the tradition of social justice, I think it must resonate that Judaism is seen as tribal — but a tribe you can join, if you try hard enough.

Learn Hebrew today and gain more than a language - gain a family

eTeacherHEBREW Join now

Try to imagine the above web ad with "Learn French..."

Marcus Hardie, an acquaintance during my time in Israel and author of the IDF memoir Black and Bulletproof, is one example from the Black side.

Hardie grew up in a gang-ridden ghetto of Los Angeles, and had already reinvented himself several times before attending law school.

BLACK & BULLETPROOF

An African-American Warrior in the Israeli Army
Marcus Hardie

He is hooked after his first Shabbat dinner, an improbable spread of every single staple of Ashkenazi cuisine:

As the chulent enters my mouth, I can feel the nutrients of the Jewish stew enter my thin body.

My stomach winks in approval.

The soup burns my throat as though carbonated or acidic. But the fluffy and light matzo balls soothe me from inside out. I'm entranced by these tiny cooked balls. I am hypnotized by the soft roundness.

Next, I reach for the gefilte fish. The round-shaped fish balls sit on the end of my fork. I lick the outside of the gefilte fish with my tongue and then gently bite down. I'm speechless.

Gefilte fish tastes like the opposite of tuna fish. It is the flip side of salmon when eaten with bitter horseradish.

I try the kugel but I hate it.

I can deal with blintz.

Eating, drinking, laughing together—all of these mundane actions are spiritual.

I begin to see my own marginalized identity as having always floated in dark corners, affected by the circumstances, media and people around me.

But racial and cultural labels suffocate my very spirit. Glancing through the prism of my spirit, I realize that black and white are just colours.

Asking a rabbi about conversion, he is told to immerse himself in the Jewish community. He volunteers at a Jewish old-age home.

Marcus, you'll make a good Jew 'cause you're a real mensch.

What's a mensch?

A mensch is a good person. It is a person who is sensitive and caring about others.

That's what Judaism is all about. If you are a mensch, then you can't go wrong.

A barg mit a barg kunnen zit nisht tzuzammen komen. Uber a mensch mit a mensch, yo.

—Two mountains cannot come together, but two people can!

Always remember that people can come together and work together.

Hardie proceeds to convert to Judaism—three times, for good measure. Reform, Conservative and Orthodox.

(He moved to Israel, like me, and served in the Armored Corps, like me. Like me, he's back on this continent. But that's another story.)

I get a feeling that my own **mother** converted and married my Jewish **father** to escape the implications of being **White** in America.

Well no, first I converted to Baptist. I decided to be a fundamentalist Christian in third grade.

My parents were vocal atheists, but we lived in the projects in northern Ohio, and mostly we were like everybody else there.

My father was an alcoholic and mostly out of work.

So church at first was a way to get out of the house. In the neighbourhood, they had camps and youth groups for free. My oldest brother went to church to play basketball.

PLAY WITH YOUR FRIENDS AND LEARN A LITTLE BIBLE

But I really believed, for awhile. If we tried hard enough, we could change the world! Make the world a better place!

But my doubts got worse as I was entering high school. Fundamentalist Christians don't believe that Catholics go to heaven. By this time, my sister married a **Catholic** and converted.

What the heck?

And what about all the people throughout history?

Like I said, my dad was an atheist. We learned the communist creed growing up. I wrote a report about Trotsky in school, I wrote on Sacco and Vanzetti. We had books all over the house.

Maybe we were a bit intellectual for the area. But everyone was blended together. I think the projects were a third each, Black, Hispanic, and White.

I'm drawn to downtrodden people, I guess. I remember a third-grade teacher who was White, but very positive towards Blacks.

She read us Uncle Remus stories, which might be a faux pas now, but I think it was a nod to the Black kids in the room. Celebrating Black storytelling.

I dated three guys in high school: one Puerto Rican and two Jews. The second Jew was your father.

I thought I might date a Black guy, but I was only interested in guys who were smarter than me. There were no Black guys in my honours classes. That must have been a failure of the system.

After I started dating your father, I got to be closer with his sister. She was actually the one who introduced me to James Baldwin. And she was younger than me!

I decided if she read it, I had to read it too. Then I really loved him.

There was a day in high school—I don't remember if it was the Watts riots or after Martin Luther King was killed. I wasn't there, I was on a YWCA trip to see the covered bridges.

Anyway, all the Black students had a sit-in, and disrupted school. It wasn't violent, but it was like we couldn't be friends anymore. It was like Blacks hated Whites.

Before, we thought of Blacks as the sports, the music and youth culture.

It was getting more acceptable, Blacks were cool, and you almost wanted to be Black, and then... stop.

After that, they were mad at us because we killed Martin Luther King, and we were mad at them because Los Angeles was on fire.

It was very **sad**. Your father was **also** upset.

I feel like it took another **ten** to fifteen years to get it **back** to where it was before King was killed.

I was interested in Judaism before I started dating your father. My first Jewish boyfriend's family was very welcoming. They invited me to their Passover.

His mother always included me. Actually I ended up liking his mother more than him.

The Seder was really educational, and of course, it's all about justice and freedom.

Judaism solved the problem of Baptist heaven. You don't have to accept Judaism to go to heaven. There's seven Noahide laws, and if you're over on those, you're ok.

God will judge each person.

In the projects, there was some prejudice against Jews. They were seen as clannish. From my father's communist perspective, Jews are bad, they're rich and capitalist.

In recessions, the Jews never suffered as bad as the rest of us.

When I was dating your father and decided to convert, my mother said,

If you're such a peacenik, and an internationalist, why would you go to this religion that's so exclusive?

That's why I wasn't attracted to Orthodox Judaism, at first. There **is** exclusion and there **is** clannishness, and it **does** bother me.

When I converted, the rabbi asked me,

Would you go back to being Christian?

If I wasn't accepted, I would go back.

I guess I never felt that I wasn't accepted.

She never speaks of Jewish **victimhood**, only Jewish **responsibility**.

I grew up feeling our **first** kinship and allegiance was to **Jews**, but our **second** was to **all** people of colour, Blacks, Hispanics, etc., with White people coming only **third**.

My **siblings** and I were the only ones who got pulled out of **school** to go to a march against **police brutality** following the **Rodney King** beating.

It's why I feel so **positively** towards this interpretation of a voluntarily **embraced** Jewish identity: a **critique** of binary oppositions and a **subversion** of their inevitability by being neither a **subaltern** nor a hegemonic **oppressor**, but a **third** way of living in relation to others...

Let's call it the **alter-altern**.

If there are any solutions to intra-Israeli racism, or Black-Jewish distrust elsewhere in the world, I think they include the (re)claiming of an alter-altern "diasporic" identity by Jews—

—from non-racially-marked Israelis (Ashkenazim, some Mizrahim and some Russians), to "visible minority" Israelis (the rest),—

—to all Jews around the world. (And whoever **else** has a use for it!)

It can include seeing yourself as 1: a racial and cultural minority, 2: meek, 3: refined, 4: brainy, 5: an ally to all other oppressed minorities.

Meek (in a proud kinda way) is already part of the stereotype of Ethiopian-Israelis, and their positive self-identity.

The wise man bows low to the great lord and silently farts.

Ethiopian Proverb

But let's also incorporate other attributes claimed by American Jews: an overanalytical neurosis, a constant questioning, a lack of complacence, even a guilt.

Philip Roth disparaged "muscular Judaism" when it began to catch on in American consciousness. He reacted in particular to the success of the 1960 feel-good Zionist shoot-em-up flick *Exodus*.

At this point in human history, when power seems the ultimate end of government, and "success" the goal of individual lives; when the value of humility is in doubt, and the nerve to fail hardly seen at all, when a wilful blindness of man's condition can only precipitate further anguishes...

I cannot help but believe that there is a higher moral purpose for the Jewish people than public relations.

P. Roth

126

It's when we let our self-doubt go, like in the fallout of 1967, that we give into the ease of being victors or victims.

"It is no longer possible for Negro intellectuals to deal with the Jewish question purely on the basis of brotherhood, compassion, morality, and other subjective responses, which rule out objective criticism." Harold Cruse, 1969

American Jews took an equal "with us or against us" posture (American Jews' Israeli "us," like Black militants' pan-third-world "us" were half a planet away, not giving a fuck about American race relations), and Jews largely dropped out of civil rights in favour of "supporting Israel."

The most important element in this alternative diasporic identity, then, is another thing that Blacks and Jews taught each other in the early 20th century: transcendent empathy.

Martin Luther King, Jr., though passionate about the struggles of his **own** people, never lost sight of the suffering of others, be they poor Whites, Vietnamese, or Jews.

The essence of a Jew is his involvement in the plight of other people, as God is involved.

I cannot stand idly **by**, even though I live in the United States and even though I **happen** to be an American Negro, and fail to be concerned about what happens to my brothers and sisters who **happen** to be Jews in Soviet Russia.

Abraham Joshua Heschel is a parallel example to Dr. King: a Polish refugee whose family was killed in the Holocaust, but who was able to draw analogies between Jewish and Black suffering.

This despite the fact that he was closer to first-hand oppression than many subsequent Black Separatist leaders who felt the need to purify their ranks of non-Blacks, and draw lines dictating whose suffering they **could** and **couldn't** acknowledge.

"Stokely Carmichael's [graduate of a prestigious, largely Jewish school in New York] election to SNCC chairman in 1966 marked the final displacement of southern Black activists by northern Blacks, who saw the former as moderate and lacking political sophistication." Clayborne Carson

He used his scholarship and his spiritual leadership to transcend Jewish parochialism in his call for welcoming the stranger as the prime mission of contemporary Jews.

The **best** articulator of a stranger-welcoming identity is the philosopher **Emanuel Levinas**, another Jew who fled Nazi Eastern Europe, finding refuge in France.

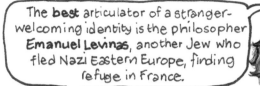

A post-Heideggerian and friend of early postmodernists, he stood out by putting an **ethical** imperative at the core of his study of **being**. He took not only welcoming the stranger, but an all-too-literal "love thy **neighbour** as **thyself**" as the basis of human existence.

Levinas on **empathy** as that which makes **morality** possible, and violence **impossible**:

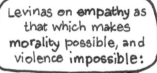

In reality, murder is **possible**, but only when one has **not** looked the Other in the **face**.

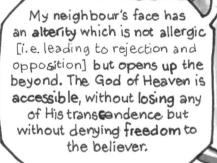

My neighbour's face has an **alterity** which is not allergic [i.e. leading to rejection and opposition] but opens up the beyond. The God of Heaven is **accessible**, without losing any of His transcendence but without denying **freedom** to the believer.

Only the vision of the **face** in which the "You shall not kill" is articulated does not allow itself to fall **back** into **complacency** or become the experience of an insuperable **obstacle**, offering itself up to our **power**.

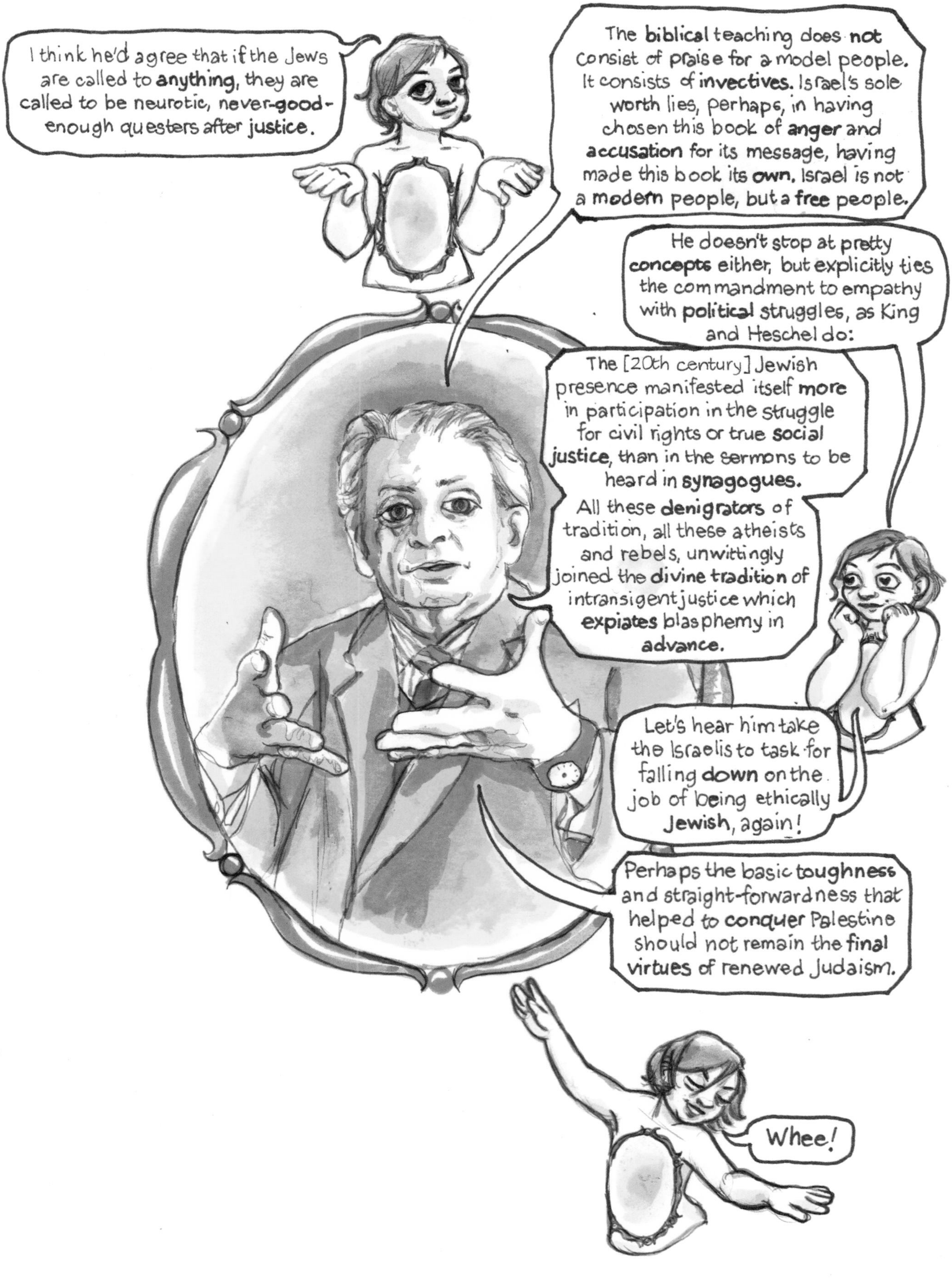
I think he'd agree that if the Jews are called to anything, they are called to be neurotic, never-good-enough questers after justice.
The biblical teaching does not consist of praise for a model people. It consists of invectives. Israel's sole worth lies, perhaps, in having chosen this book of anger and accusation for its message, having made this book its own. Israel is not a modern people, but a free people.
He doesn't stop at pretty concepts either, but explicitly ties the commandment to empathy with political struggles, as King and Heschel do:
The [20th century] Jewish presence manifested itself more in participation in the struggle for civil rights or true social justice, than in the sermons to be heard in synagogues.
All these denigrators of tradition, all these atheists and rebels, unwittingly joined the divine tradition of intransigent justice which expiates blasphemy in advance.
Let's hear him take the Israelis to task for falling down on the job of being ethically Jewish, again!
Perhaps the basic toughness and straight-forwardness that helped to conquer Palestine should not remain the final virtues of renewed Judaism.
Whee!

Part IX: Strangeing the Welcomer

Me, I got interested in this subject for the same reasons any White American Jew does. The Beta Israel seemed so beautiful and exotic.

But radical empathy is not the same as generally having warm feelings towards people, and it's easier said than done.

In Levinas, facing is being confronted with, turned towards, facing up to, being judged and called to by the other. Facing is a disruption of that free, autonomous self which [through its reasoning and consciousness] thinks it can construct the world out of itself, or know the world from itself.

Susan Handelman

krik

krak

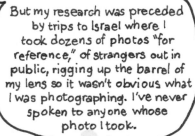

In this essay, I wanted to give Ethiopian Israelis the respect of not speaking for them; what, beyond statistics and anecdotes, their lives might be like, or what they feel about things.

But my research was preceded by trips to Israel where I took dozens of photos "for reference," of strangers out in public, rigging up the barrel of my lens so it wasn't obvious what I was photographing. I've never spoken to anyone whose photo I took.

ksshhh

"Failing to face the Other" doesn't get more literal than that.

After our three-week basic training was over, I never saw Sarah (Satuy) again. Actually, we barely spoke to each other after those hours in the guard tower.

That night was the longest conversation I've ever had with an Ethiopian Israeli.

whoops...

So what strategies do Ethiopian-Israelis **have** for escaping the suffocating "**Other**" box??

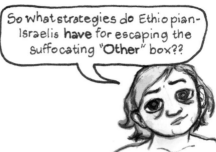

EXOTIC
TRADITIONAL
"A COMMUNITY IN DISTRESS"

NOT LIKE US
UNCIVILIZED
WELFARE CASES

Some analysts look at the **Bob Marley** t-shirts and the **Ethiopian dance** clubs and see the **substituting** of pan-**African** identity for a Jewish one.

The young people go to clubs that are meant mainly for **them**. So they **continue** the segregation processes, this time at their own will. The reggae and rap, the clothes and the hairstyles that match their status offer them a haven from the categorizations that marginalize them.

Have these young people found a solution to their situation by replacing skullcaps with **dreadlocks**?

Uri Ben-Eliezer

So "**Black pride**" **reinforces** the difference between Ethiopian Israelis and "**Israelis**," and makes everyday racism **more** possible, and **integration** less probable.

In dance clubs, Ethiopian youth encounter a non-formal separation policy. "Go to your own discotheques," they are told by the security guards. The fact that they indeed have their own discotheques, and music and unique dances, gives the guards an excuse to treat them not as "Israelis" but as "Ethiopians."

Saying that growing **dreadlocks** doesn't **help** integration begs the question, though, of whether shaving your hair **army-short** (or straightened, or "traditional" braids, or whatever the Jewish way is to style African hair) would **help** the cause of integration—

—Or whether Israeli **racism** exerts its power **irrespective** of multicultural identities.

It may be relevant to **note** that as I creepily trawled through Internet images of Ethiopian-Israeli kids at nightclubs for my illustrations, I had a very hard time finding boys who **didn't** style themselves exactly like all **other** secular Israelis their age: buzzed hair, tight polos, artfully-distressed tight jeans.

Sure, a lot of the **girls** were channeling **Rihanna**, but who **wouldn't**, if they could get away with it?

Seriously.

I would.

131

One of the (very) few sociological studies coauthored by an Ethiopian-Israeli found that aside from a wealthy, educated elite, Ethiopians preferred to identify with Jews ahead of a global African diaspora.

Adane Zawdu   Nissim Mizrachi

Most also opposed affirmative action, and analogized the prejudice they faced to prejudice faced by earlier immigrations, including the Mizrahim.

Every immigrant group suffered, in turn. So we've suffered **more**, but it's **temporary.** It's something you can overcome and continue **on.**

"Shlomo," anonymous Ethiopian-Israeli respondent

It's really up to you, how you view yourself. In the beginning, it seems **strange** to them that someone **black** is standing before them.

But you have to be **sure** of yourself; you have to **argue.** You shouldn't feel **inferior.**

"Vered," ibid.

Mass protests in the last ten years, rather than showing that Ethiopian Israelis want to **estrange** themselves from the mainstream, mean they have **embraced** an Israeli **mindset**—where you have to "**stick out your elbows**," and **kvetching** is the only way to bring about **change.**

Ethiopian youth are more drawn into crime than ten years ago. But they are **also** more committed to **education** and self-help, as seen from the community leaders on the **seventh** page.

Now it's **Israel's** turn to change.

Part X: Black and White and Jews All Over

The aforementioned study defined two choices: **nationalism** (pride in "Ethiopianness" at the expense of acquiring Israeli identity) or **universalism** (a claim that we are all **equal**, carrying the risk of devaluing the uniqueness of Ethiopian Israelis' **household** culture). This is not just the choice presented to Ethiopian-Israeli youth, but to **all** of us.

PICK ONE

Claiming **subaltern** status, though useful sometimes, is a kind of **complacency** and an easy way out of hard **questions** just as perpetuating (White or Ashkenazi) **supremacy** is.

Radical **empathy** and alter-alterity, where you view yourself through others' eyes rather than as the norm, is the moral challenge that keeps on giving.

What if we **all** chose the path between pride and self-erasure, the path of radical empathy and self-examination which breaks through metanarratives? Maybe then we'd welcome all strangers as more than simulacra. Maybe, as per **King, Heschel**, and **Levinas**, we'd see the infinite in each person, and the violence of dehumanization would be impossible.

Racism is not a **biological** concept. It shuts people away in a **class**, deprives them of expression, and condemns them to being signifiers without a signified, and from there to violence and fighting.

How can we deliver a message about our **humanity** from behind the bars of quotation marks?

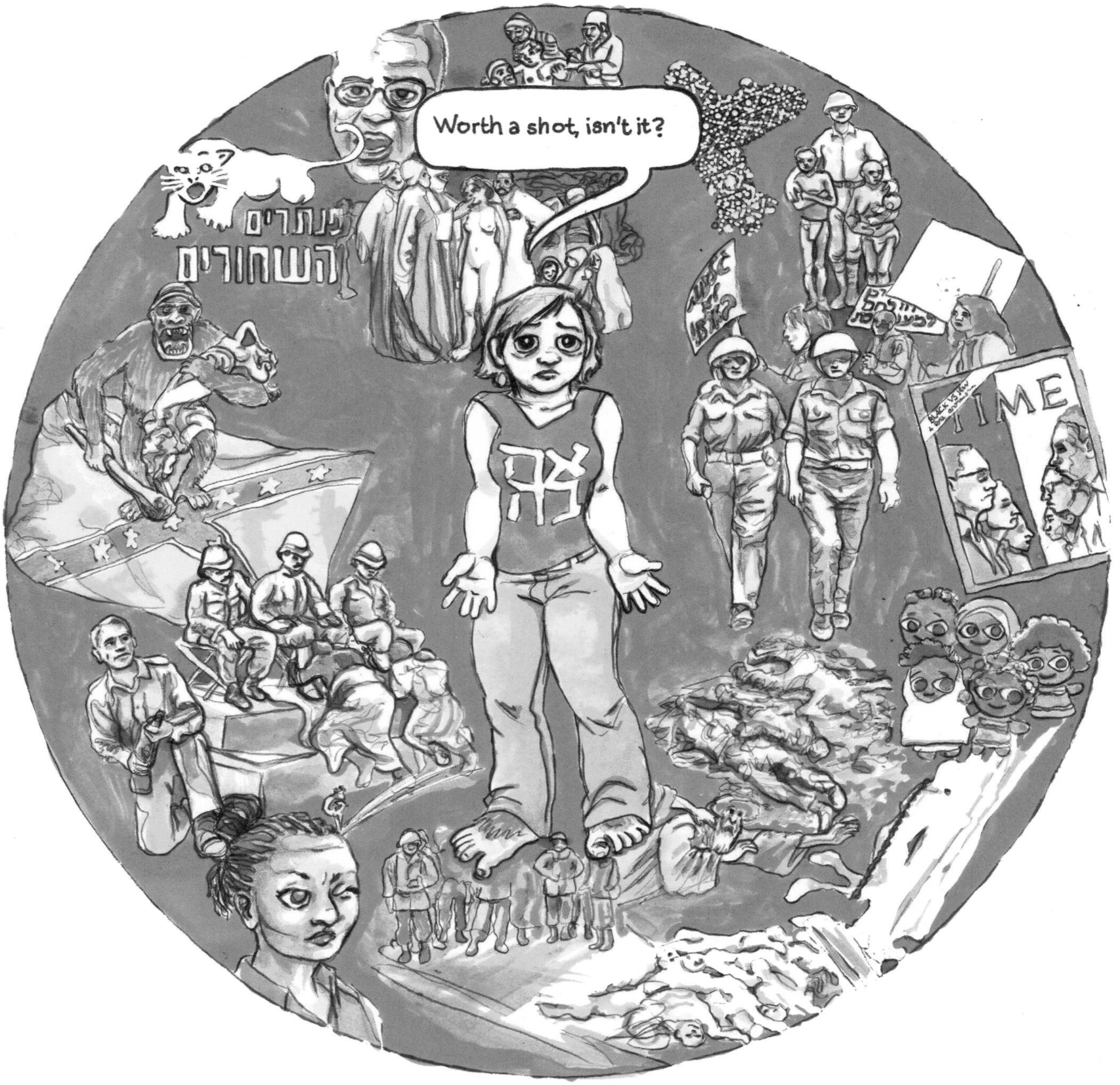
Worth a shot, isn't it?
פנתרים
השחורים
TIME
BLACK VS JEW

THANK YOU:

My humanities mentors: Ranen Omer-Sherman, Janice Fernheimer, Lou Schubert. I would be a lot more wrong if it weren't for you (any wrongness remaining is all mine). Gary Groth, for scaring me shitless at first but secretly believing in me for the last ten years. My parents, who always challenge me to use my brain and my heart, and endlessly tolerate where those lead me. My comix family, especially but not limited to: Keef, Stephen, Devon, Josh, Rachel, Mikey, Justin and Hillary. I would have given up cartooning ten years ago if I hadn't found you. My best friends/second readers/shoulders to cry on: Naomi, Tamar, Vanessa, James, Clara, Matthew. You make things make sense outside my head. My kids: Mered and Migdal. You slow me down but you also make every day worth it. And Mike Yoshioka: you make my life stable enough to create, you drag my lazy ass to cons, you mostly like superheroes but you support my comix anyway.